SIMPLE
IS
POWERFUL

Anecdotes
for a Complex World

Michael J. Roads

H J Kramer Inc
Tiburon, California

H J Kramer Inc
P.O. Box 1082
Tiburon, CA 94920

Editor: Doris Ober
Cover Art: T. Taylor Bruce
Cover Design: Spectra Media
Editorial Assistant: Nancy Grimley Carleton
Book Production: Schuettge and Carleton
Typesetting: Classic Typography
Manufactured in the United States of America
10 9 8 7 6 5 4 3 2 1

Library of Congress Cataloging-in-Publication Data

Roads, Michael J.
  Simple is powerful : anecdotes for a complex world / Michael J.
Roads.
     p.   cm.
  ISBN 0-915811-35-9
  1. Simplicity. 2. Homeland Foundation Community (Australia)
3. Roads, Michael J. 4. Roads, Treenie. I. Title.
BJ1496.R63   1991
179'.9—dc20   91-52848
                                                         CIP

To my beloved Treenie,
a lady of great power
and simplicity.

*The characters
mentioned in this
book are real people, most
still alive, some have passed on.
I have changed the names
only where I consider
it necessary.*

M.J.R.

Contents

Contents

Acknowledgments

As always, my thanks first of all are to Treenie. This book was her idea, and she persuaded me to write it. "We want a book to empower everybody," she said, "and it must be simple." Hopefully, she got her wish!

Linda Kramer has just as much insight in recognizing a simple and powerful book. My sincere thanks, Sis!

To Hal Kramer, my publisher and friend, thank you and Linda both for giving form and clarity to my words.

To Doris Ober, my editor, my very sincere thanks. Taking my theme literally, she used her considerable skills with a deft and simple touch to make my written words even stronger.

To those people who are mentioned in this book—relatives, friends, and people who touched my life, all part of one human family—my very deepest thanks.

Introduction

This book is one of smiles, chuckles, and a deep, thought-provoking hmmmm. I mean it to be a simple book, but not simplistic. I hope it reveals that simplicity is powerful, and that within each one of us there exists a simple but profound inner knowledge. This is our place of power—a wonderful place from which to live, to redesign our lives, to express our wisdom.

As you read these pages, you may recognize yourself, for each of us faces the same challenges; each of us laughs at the same ridiculous things we do and say; each cries over the same hurts and fears.

For most of us, life is busy, busy, busy. The daily rush as a commuter is a trial of nerves, the pace and problems of work a daily pressure; the intricacies of family life consume any spare time we get. We have become very complex, and at the same time, complexed.

This complexity takes away our ability to express and be who we truly are, rather than a stressed and devalued shadow self. We have become so busy, so pressured, so very complexed in the overall haste of life, we have forgotten that simple is powerful.

This book is a reminder.

Oh, and my references to Oz are, of course, Australia.

1

The Swing of Things

Have you ever noticed that life is always giving us simple messages? So simple, in fact, we seldom notice them. We forget that simple is powerful.

A couple of years ago, I reached my fiftieth year *and* became a grandfather. I was rapt! I had yet to learn how much a tiny child could teach me. I had the idea that as a grandfather I would be her mentor, and so I will, but I had to learn that it is a two-way process.

One windy afternoon when my wife Treenie and I were visiting Adrian and Jo, our son and daughter-in-law and proud parents of Abbey, now two years old, I decided to take Abbey for a walk to the shops. Although she dislikes walking, preferring to be carried, Jo insisted it would be better for Abbey to walk. I promised her that we would spend some time in the local park where she could have a swing. She loves swings.

It didn't take much to cajole Abbey into the walk, which I knew was basically for my own gratification, and away we went. Now, people can dawdle, but a two-year-old can turn dawdling into a fine art. As we ambled along the back streets, past old, terraced houses with bold new face-lifts in this newly trendy area, I found myself gradually becoming impatient. Jo had warned me that Abbey was slow, but I thought she exaggerated. I had envisaged Abbey running at my side, eager and happy to be going to the park. But it didn't work out that way.

Abbey stopped at every flower poking from its inner-city garden, stared at it from half a dozen different angles, tried to pick it, touched each petal in turn, all while I slowly simmered. And there were hundreds of flowers!

Each crack in the pavement had to be either carefully negotiated or followed, regardless of which direction it went. Have you ever noticed the house fences in an older part of the city? No? Well, walk past them with a two-year-old! One particular iron-railing fence had a small, misshapen gargoyle molded into each support post. Having tapped every single rail with a stick as we crawled past it, Abbey reached the first gargoyle.

All progress ceased. I thought I was in touch with the twelve-year-old in me, but there is a whole world between twelve and two. Abbey's conversation with each gargoyle can never be recorded, for it was held in a language that strictly excludes all other age groups, but she was enthralled. It took me nearly twenty minutes to get her past six gargoyles!

The gargoyles rather brought things to a head. I couldn't decide whether it was a deliberate ploy by Abbey to force me to carry her and thus win in this battle of wills, or if she genuinely found the gargoyles so captivating.

It was at this stage I tried bribery, the usual adult cop-out. With the promise of a chocolate Freddo Frog dangling like a carrot before her, I increased our pace from a flat-out nothing to merely very slow!

Eventually we reached the shops, the bribe was paid,

and I watched with fascination as this two-year-old managed to spread one small packaged chocolate frog across her entire face, all over her cardigan, and even have some left for my hands. I had forgotten kids could do that.

After I made sure we were taking a road with no more mute gargoyles, we made our way slowly to the park where the swings awaited. I repeat, Abbey loves swings. Not slides, not merry-go-rounds, not playing on the grass — but swings! I pushed her back and forth on her favorite swing for maybe ten minutes before I suggested a go on the merry-go-round. No! She wanted to swing.

"You've been swinging," I said. "How about a slide?"

"More swing." Direct and to the point, no room for negotiation. So, more swings it was.

While Abbey swung and I idly pushed, I glanced around at the other adults. With a single exception, they all looked bored and glum. I knew why. Each accompanied a small child, and while the child swung or merry-go-rounded or slid, the parent looked bored. One business-suited man looked particularly glum. He sat on a park bench, basically ignoring the boy of three or four who played nearby. The kid raced over to where Abbey was swinging, then ran around the swings, laughing out loud, exuberant.

"What are you doing?" I asked him.

"Having fun," he replied.

I glanced at his father. "Is that your dad?"

"Yes."

"Where's your mum?"

"At home."

"Is Dad supposed to be playing with you?"

3

"Yes."

I glanced again at the immobile father, his face lost in the depths of thoughts that totally occupied him.

"But you're having fun anyway?"

"Oh, yes," and away he went, racing around the swinging Abbey. Then leaving us, he ran across to his father, trying vainly to catch his attention.

I glanced again at the other people in this small, windy park: an elderly couple, looking rather defeated by life, and the other parents, each with a child. A young woman laughed and played with her little girl, but from the rest — boredom.

Where did I fit in? The question hit me suddenly. I became aware of my own expression. It was serious; I certainly wasn't laughing.

Yet the small boy was having fun, despite Dad. I looked at the other kids, and they were all either totally engrossed in their play, or laughing. I looked at Abbey, her red hair blowing in the wind, cheeks glowing, blue eyes innocent and piercing; she laughed at me. No reason to laugh, but she was having fun.

I made an inner shift. The answer was obvious. The kids were in the moment — and loving it, but we adults were somewhere else in our heads. Our bodies were in the park, but we were somewhere else. We weren't having fun! Fun is an art. Fun is making the most of what is available. Fun isn't sophisticated entertainment; fun is being with life in the moment. Fun is simple, and powerful.

From that moment I was *with* Abbey, swinging her swing, playing her games, and loving them. I swung her as high as the swing could go without completing an arc, and she shrieked her glee. Her eyes held mine and we laughed together. We walked the long way home and I talked to the flowers, counted their petals, and picked a few. I learned the gargoyle language, muttering my own magical words of power, and I followed the cracks in the pavement, no matter where they led us.

When we were nearly home, I picked Abbey up and, snuggling close to me, her red hair tickling my nose, she talked her mystical words into my ear. I didn't want it to end, not yet, so I turned back, walking right around the block again with her in my arms.

It was so simple. We all won. I had my walk, and Abbey got carried just as she had wanted. And nobody knew how much I had wanted to carry and cuddle her. I also got educated. I learned that fun happens right *now*, and I was taught by a mentor with all the right qualifications!

2

A Harmless Story

Have you ever thought about harmlessness? I hadn't, until life showed me an example. It was a bittersweet experience because I learned that some things cannot be forced, or coerced, or manipulated.

It all came about quite simply. With a few friends, I had made plans for a day's walk through some dense jungle that forested the steep escarpment surrounding our local valley. This involved a drive to the very end of the valley, followed by a clamber through the wonders of the rain forest. There was only one catch. A reclusive family lived at the far end of the valley, and to walk where we wanted to go meant passing through their property.

By all accounts they were a pretty wild mob. Rumor had it that two sisters lived there amicably with the same man, each rearing a brood of children. Some of those kids were now in their late teens, and rumor said that anyone caught trespassing had a rough time.

So, just to be on the safe side, we drove to the far end of the valley, parked our car, and headed straight for the distant farmhouse. It was just as well. There was no way we could have avoided the pack of dogs that met us, all barking and snarling as though we were destined for dog meat. Maybe it was all bluff, for we remained unbitten during the walk, and when the alerted family met us, we were cordially invited inside.

The two ladies offered us tea, for clearly they wanted to chat. Most of the kids, large and small, left us alone, but I noticed one boy, probably in his late teens, sidle over to the far end of the room. He looked as rough as the rest, but something about him attracted my attention. Whenever I caught his eye, he looked away, almost cringing, and I soon realized that he suffered a mild mental retardation.

Neither he nor I really followed the conversation. He wanted to get away from my scrutiny, and I wondered what it was about him that tugged at my attention. Crabwise, he slid past me, his eyes carefully averted, before scuttling out of the room. Curious, I followed him, keeping myself inconspicuous.

As soon as he was outside and away from people, his whole posture changed. Gone was the cringe, his shoulders straightened. And then it happened.

A bird flew down from a nearby bush, alighting on his arm. He paid it only casual attention, but it was a fantail, not a magpie or some other easily tamed bird. As I watched, two more fantails flitted around him, then a cocky male blue wren, his colors bright and cheeky.

I stared in awe. It was like something out of a Disney animated movie. Leaving their mothers grazing in a nearby field, three calves romped over to him, to be joined by two lambs. As a final touch of magic, eight dogs hung almost on the young man's heels, now quiet and passive and gazing at him in obvious adoration. Even more ridiculous was the fact that all the animals and birds were totally tolerant

8

of each other. I knew, without any doubt, that this young-ster was the center of the harmony.

He was talking to the birds and other animals, his words a litany of nonsense to my ears, but obviously an endear-ment to them. Then he looked up suddenly and our eyes met. Two things happened simultaneously. Embarrassed, he trotted away, complete with the birds flying around his head and the motley mass of animals—and, with a flash of insight, I understood. That young man was blessed with harmlessness!

I mean real harmlessness.

Big deal, you may be thinking, but think again. Do you know anyone who is so harmless that no *thought* of spite or offense ever even enters his or her mind!

Don't ask me how I knew. Insight is not intellectual; it's intuitive. I just knew. It may have helped that I had tried for years to express my own harmlessness with wild birds and animals, but I had always failed. I have shot too many animals in the past, too many birds. I wear that in my con-sciousness like a badge, and all those so-called dumb ani-mals and birds can read it, easily.

I never forgot that young man. Society would label him mentally handicapped. I can't help thinking that society has the handicap; we humans cannot read our own silent messages. We easily fool each other, but Nature, no way!

Probably no animals illustrate this more aptly than our own domestic pets. My wife Treenie and I have some close friends, Mike and Rosemary, who used to own a black, shaggy-haired pooch named Nicky. Nicky was your average, easygoing, ultraharmless, superfriendly mutt who offered the ultimate danger of licking you to death! He was one of those dogs that wag their tails endlessly, such was his outgoing friendliness.

The story I am about to tell was reconstructed by Mike and Rosemary from fairly obvious evidence and noises later reported by neighbors.

The television had been on for several hours when Mike gave Nicky his usual bedtime call at around ten o'clock in the evening. It was Nicky's routine to prowl the garden and close locality at the end of the day. About half an hour later, Mike realized that Nicky had not yet come in for bed. He called again. Another fifteen minutes passed, but no dog.

Concerned, Mike and Rosemary went looking for Nicky and were shocked to find him lying in a pool of his own blood, scarcely breathing, one eye hanging by a thread of tissue from its socket. They rushed him to the local veterinary hospital for emergency treatment.

What the pieced-together evidence indicated was this: At approximately half past nine, a burglar had tried to gain entry, using one of the windows at the far end of the house. Under cover of the television noise, he (presumably a he!) had used a heavy iron bar to attempt to pry open a window. Incredibly, Nicky had attacked him. Neighbors heard a scuffle and then the man must have hit Nicky over the head, knocking him stunned and bleeding to the ground.

The man apparently continued in his efforts to gain entry, transferring his attention to a different window. Meanwhile, Nicky recovered, and, once again following his instinct to defend his owners from the intruder, attacked.

Again the man lashed out, this time smashing the dog a terrible blow across the skull and eye before he ran away, leaving Nicky unconscious and dying.

The good news is — Nicky lived. He lost his eye, but never his friendly, outgoing nature. The point of the story is this: Nicky knew the burglar's *intent* was one of harm. He read it in the energy of the man. It was not the action of trying to get in the window that aroused the dog but the *intent* behind it. If I had attempted to get in that same window Nicky might well have tried to help me. He would have known that my intent was beneficial to the family, not harmful.

We are seldom intuitive enough to know the intent of those around us, or of those with whom we deal in business. If only we could read those inner, silent messages, think of the grief and suffering we could avoid, the terrible misunderstandings. Yet a simple mongrel dog read them with ease.

There is a rather nice epilogue to this story. About nine years later, when Nicky was around sixteen years old and showing his age, Mike and Rosemary were considering whether to get a puppy to replace Nicky when he died. Both were thinking about a red kelpie, but neither had mentioned that to the other.

One night when their youngest son Justin went to bed, he heard some scuffling in the shrubs near his bedroom window. Mike checked it out, but found nothing. Only a few minutes later, Justin called again, "Dad, there *is* something outside. I heard it."

Mike checked once more and found nothing.

An hour passed and Justin called, "I heard it again, Dad. Something's there."

Grumbling and muttering, Mike went back to the garden to look for prowlers, but once again drew a blank.

"Go to sleep, Justin. If there's anything out there, it's just a toad."

Knowing that cane toads were abundant in their area, this satisfied Justin and he went to sleep.

In the morning, Mike looked for footprints, or any evidence of a prowler around the windows. Instead, he found a small, shivering, abandoned puppy—a red kelpie!

Naturally, they adopted him. Nicky welcomed the newcomer and trained him in the art of defending the home and caring for the humans in his family. About two months later, Nicky died peacefully, his duty fulfilled.

Of course, Mike and Rosemary named the puppy Toad!

3

Warts and All

Have you ever noticed how we frequently dwell on what can go wrong, and seldom on what can go right? The negative seems to stand out so strongly, while the positive meekly hides. Maybe it's simply that the negative aspects of life tend to shout at us, while the positive aspects whisper.

Quite a number of years ago, I was involved in an incident that demonstrates this. In hindsight, the story is funny, but at the time it contained little humor. It began one morning while I was shaving. I was contorting my face into the usual grimaces that shaving requires, when I noticed a small wart on the end of my nose. In those days, I had a fair investment of self-worth in how I appeared to the world at large. Generally I was not unhappy with my face, but I had no desire for a wart on the end of my nose.

I studied it carefully. It had not been there yesterday when I shaved—or had it? I couldn't decide whether it had sneaked up over the past couple of days, unnoticed, or whether it was a sudden, overnight job. Not that it made much difference.

It was hate at first sight. More than anything, I was offended by its precise geometrical position—without doubt, if calipers had been used, the wart could not have been centered more perfectly on the tip of my nose.

I finished shaving, glaring at the wart as though sheer force of will might shrink it to nothing. It did not! After some contemplation, I decided on a wait-and-see tactic. Maybe it would disappear as easily as it had appeared.

Two weeks later, I had to concede that this very small yet hugely offensive wart was here to stay. I waited another week, then another, before deciding on swift and drastic action.

I went to the local chemist shop and bought a small caustic stick with a silver nitrate coating. I was well aware of the potency of a caustic stick. Once, when I was about ten years old, I had collected a wart on the back of my neck. That one had not bothered me at all, except when I went to the barber and his hand clipper clipped the wart. That had bothered me!

I told Mum and she bought a silver nitrate caustic stick. That night, she carefully applied it just before I went to bed, but she forgot that I was an Aries. Convinced that she hadn't used enough of the miracle stick, I sneaked quietly into the bathroom and, using a hand-held mirror to see the back of my neck, I clumsily applied a liberal coating to the whole general area. Then I went back to bed, satisfied.

I woke up in the middle of the night with a burning sensation on the back of my neck. I switched on the bedside light. There was blood everywhere. It was all over the pillow, on my hands, my face. Everywhere the caustic stick had been applied was raw flesh. I was a real mess, and I hurt!

That's how I learned about the potency of silver nitrate. So now, an adult with a small wart on a very accessible nose, I intended to be ultracareful.

I applied the tip of the caustic stick to that rotten little wart with a mixed sense of glee and apprehension.

A couple of days later, my morning shave revealed that the wart had dropped off. I was overjoyed!

All went well for three weeks, when one morning I noticed a wart on the precise center of the tip of my nose! It was back and — horror on horror — it was now double its original size. I stared at it, appalled.

Once again I tried the wait-and-see method, and once again it took only a couple of weeks for the wart to demonstrate that it had no intention of leaving. With great care, I again applied the caustic stick.

A couple of mornings later I was wart free.

Then came another fateful morning. The wart was back — and it had doubled in size again! I stared at it aghast. Now what? This wart, once so small, was now easily noticeable. With only the faintest effort, I could squint down the length of my nose and see the wart, rather like a horrendous biological gun sight! I groaned in dismay.

By now I was convinced that everyone was staring at it. I found myself apologizing to people for the wart on the end of my nose, and their amusement did nothing for my vanity. I endured about a month in a constant state of embarrassment.

My dilemma was acute. Did I wear it for life, or should I make one more attempt with the caustic stick? Eventually, vanity won. After this application, I was wart free for seven weeks.

When the wart returned this time it had doubled its size again. I no longer had to squint down my nose to see it. It waved at me.

Life now became full-on misery. I no longer shaved a face, I shaved around a wart. When I talked to friends, I held my hand over my nose in a casual way as though I were scratching my face, but all such tactics failed miserably. When I moved my hand, there would be an exclamation, followed by, "Oh look! Did you know you've got a wart on the tip of your nose?"

What a fool of a question. I began to avoid people. One thing was absolutely certain—I no longer dared apply the caustic stick. If the wart doubled in size again it would make a takeover bid for my nose! (Silly as it sounds, I did not think of going to a doctor during all this. I was so anti-doctors at that time it did not occur to me.)

It did not help that Treenie regarded the whole affair as a lot of fuss about nothing. "I love you, my darling," she said with exaggerated humor, "warts and all!"

I endured that wart in a miserable hate affair for several more weeks, until one calm sunny day I went down to our river. The water was still, rather like a placid pool, and as I glanced into its depths, my reflection shimmered on the water's surface as on a fogged mirror. I could see my face, but without enough detail to show the wart. What a blessed relief.

I gazed at my rippling reflection. How I hated that wart. Why did I have it? Why had it suddenly appeared?

Probably the calm of the river influenced me, because for a while I was quiet inside—and from that quiet welled hidden questions.

What was my focus when I looked in the mirror? Did I see my face as a whole, or just the isolated wart?

Was it possible that my focus in life had become centered on the negative? A few minutes of painfully honest self-scrutiny revealed it was very possible.

Was it possible that I, a seeker of truth, was physically acting out a truth I sought? It made so much sense if I considered myself as the positive and the wart as a negative. My attention had become so centered on the wart that I had lost sight of me.

The process now started, questions flowed, and insight followed.

Did I see any beauty in my face at all? No. I had developed tunnel vision. I saw only the ugliness of a wart.

Treenie's words came back to me. "I love you, my darling, warts and all."

Could I do that—love myself, warts and all? Could it be that simple? Was it possible that life was presenting me with an opportunity for personal growth? Could this be part of a grand design, with no other purpose than to give me a chance to consciously and knowingly "love myself"?

I left the river with a great inner excitement. I felt as though an old shadow was moving into the light—and I was the old shadow!

I walked indoors, making my way to the bathroom mirror. My reflection showed the wart still there, but . . . there was a face around it! I realized I could focus on the positive or the negative—the choice was mine.

Smiling at my own reflection, I tried to tell the wart that I loved it, but that was so clearly a lie, I could not do it. I settled for accepting the wart, but seeing it—and myself—from a whole new perspective.

Three weeks later, I woke up knowing that the wart was gone. A glance in the mirror confirmed it. And I knew why. That wart had symbolized the shout of my negativity. Treenie's lighthearted words had not only revealed my conceit, but also my inability to accept and embrace myself in a totally positive way.

I realize now how lucky I was. I wore my wart on the tip of my nose, so I couldn't help but see it—but for many people their "warts" are far less obvious. While we hide them from the world, we hide them from ourselves.

This may well be unwitting self-deceit, but it deprives us of our power. Accept yourself as you are right now—warts and all!

It's incredibly simple, but so powerful.

4

Victim of Circumstances

One of the things in life that never fails to surprise me is the impact we humans have on each other.

I remember many years ago in a large country town, taking a walk that became a lesson in life.

Walking toward me was a middle-aged man, quite nondescript, except for his face. His expression was one of complete gloom, of utter defeat, even dread. Maybe his doctor had just told him he had a terminal illness; perhaps he had a heavily overdrawn account and was on his way to see his bank manager—I will never know—but I do know he affected me adversely.

I felt my spirits drop. I suddenly felt unhappy. I could feel his energy affecting me, but I could do nothing about it. It was as though I had walked into a dark cloud, and I could not find the sun.

I passed him by, my footsteps less buoyant, not quite sure of just what had happened. I walked no more than a couple of streets farther, when a sight in front of me brought me to a stop.

Holding onto a lamppost with one huge hand, a very fat lady stood laughing with short, breathless explosions of mirth. In her other hand she held a letter, and as she screamed aloud with laughter, her body bouncing and rolling in independent layers of fat, she needed her grip on the lamppost to keep herself on her feet!

Like magic, my gloom was blown away, and I chuckled at her overflowing, overpowering hilarity.

It was only then that I realized what had happened. Two incidents, each less than fifteen minutes apart, had totally affected me, yet I knew nothing about either of the people involved. Overpowered—that was the clue. I had been unwittingly overpowered by two people.

Walking along, I had been scattered; my thoughts were a mishmash of nonsense. Had I been centered, focused in the moment, then my power would have been with me, and I would not have been a victim of all that happened around me.

Being in control of our own lives is simple, but it requires attention. If we live in a mindless fashion—and we all do sometimes—then we are more easily affected by other minds. This is not bad or wrong, just tiring! It drains our power.

Recently, my friend Ruth told me about a related experience. She had been sitting in her car waiting for her husband to come out of the bank, when a rough type of man cycled past, shouting angrily at a small dog running alongside him. When the man yelled, the dog ran around Ruth's car, jumped through the open window, and lay cowering on the floor at her feet. She patted it, then opened the door and ushered it out.

Meanwhile, the man had dismounted from his bicycle, and was again shouting abuse at the whimpering dog. Yelping, it ran around the car and jumped back in through the window.

This time the man jerked open the door, and swearing volubly, brutally hauled the poor dog out into the street.

As they disappeared, the dog's tail between its legs as it followed the bicycle, Ruth felt the full impact of her distress. Then, too late, she thought of all the things she should have said to the man, the action she should have taken.

Her real distress lay in the fact that she had been so taken aback while it all happened, she had done nothing. That night she lay awake while her mind churned it over and over. The incident had lasted less than a minute, but she felt its impact on her and her blood pressure for the rest of the day and night.

There is only one real cure for such distress, but it is so simple it is rarely practiced. Our power resides in our relationship with this moment *now*. When we slip into the past, we lose our power; we become a victim of something that is no longer real. Ruth let go of the moment of *now*, that continuity in which we live, and became the continuity of the past—reliving her moment of distress. In this way, she prolonged her trauma and suffering, creating an ordeal that in actuality had ended many hours earlier.

We don't have to be the victim of circumstances; we can master them.

I remember once, well over a decade ago, when a friend of mine told me something very insulting and scathing another friend had apparently said about me. I say apparently, because I had no proof; nevertheless, I was outraged.

Typical of an Aries, I leaped into my Land Rover and headed straight for his home, a mile or so away. I wanted a

21

direct confrontation. So keen was I to get there, I took a shortcut through the local sawmill, where Frank, the owner, waved at me to stop. Reluctantly, I applied the brakes.

Frank leaned in the window, grinning at me. "Where the hell are you going in such a hurry?" he asked. Then he saw the look on my face, and added, "What's up?"

I had a lot of respect for Frank. For me, he was a kind of mentor, and he had been around a lot longer than I. After some hesitation, I told him everything.

Frank laughed. "Is that bloody all? Fred's insulted you. So bloody what? If I went chasing after everybody who insulted me or was two-faced behind my back, I'd spend all day at it!"

I was cooling down by then, so I gave it some thought. What Frank said was true enough. As the wealthiest man with the biggest business in the area, he was the subject of veiled envy and spite. I had heard it myself, yet he shrugged it off. I have never forgotten his next words. "They're just fleas on yer back, Mike. Don't worry about it. Worry is interest paid on troubles not yet due. Forget it. Get on with today. I'm bloody sure you've got enough work to keep you occupied without chasing after someone for what they *might* have said."

I thanked him, turned the Land Rover around, and headed home. Today, I would add a few words to Frank's wisdom: Worry is interest paid on troubles not yet due. Worry is also a very taxing burden, a tax we don't have to pay.

Frank's advice was simple—and powerful.

❁   ❁   ❁

Far worse than the hastily spoken word is the impact of unspoken and sustained hostility. When I farmed in Tasmania, I met a wonderful elderly lady. She was an outrageous character, full of life and energy, yet governed by strict rules of right and wrong. Let me be clear about this. Her right did not necessarily have to be right, or her wrong, wrong, but *her* definition of right and wrong was the border and boundary of her life.

The old lady had four sons, all of them grown with families of their own. Each was a character in his own right, but Wes was far more in the mold of his mother than the others.

One day, when the old lady and I were deep in conversation, I learned that she did not speak to Wes. I asked her why. "'Cos he don't speak to me," she replied indignantly.

Around a month later I had a conversation with Wes. He was an excellent worker, but a man with a brooding, rather surly nature. With considerable care, I steered our talk around to his mother, asking him a question that could only be answered if they were on speaking terms.

"I don't rightly know," he replied. "The old lady don't speak to me."

By now I was intrigued. "Do you speak to her?" I asked.

He looked shocked. "No, of course not. I just told you, she don't speak to me."

"But why not?" I asked.

"I don't rightly know," he said.

"Why don't you ask her, then?"

"She started it, let her end it!" he replied, and with that he stalked away, looking quite offended.

23

I found an excuse to go and see the old lady again. These were all country folk, and the squawking of her hens hustling away from the Land Rover announced my arrival.

"G'day, Michael. What can I do for you?" she began, and with that we were off. She just loved to talk! Eventually, I asked her why she and Wes were not speaking.

She glared at me suspiciously. "I told you a'ready. He don't speak to me; that's why I don't speak to 'im."

"But he said the same," I expostulated. "Why don't you speak to him first, then he will talk to you."

I thought she would explode, she was so angry. "He started it," she shouted, "so he can end it."

Over the months that followed, I persisted in interfering. I learned that neither mother nor son had the faintest idea of why or how their silence had started. Talk about victims of circumstance, yet this circumstance was of their own creation. I even tried to reconcile them, but that proved impossible. Each had decided that the other had done something "wrong," and each punished the other with silence.

When the old lady died six years later, mother and son had remained locked in mute hostility for ten years. Ten years of life each denied the other. That's impact! All either of them had to do was be the first to speak, the first to forgive. The first to say I'm sorry or I love you.

How impossibly simple is that?

5

The Ability to Respond

For many years I have been interested in personal freedom. Among other things, this means surrendering all the little idiosyncratic habits that make up and rule my life. Becoming free does not come easily. I've had to work at it. Habits have a habit of hanging on.

Of all the different habits we pick up, I think reacting must be the most powerful. To me, there is a world of difference between reaction and response. When we react, we don't think; we are involved in a generally instinctive reflex action, which is basically a reenactment of the past. It *always* comes from our past. Often, one person's reaction sets off a chain reaction among others.

Response is the opposite of reaction. To respond, we must be consciously involved in the moment. Generally, we react when threatened, and respond when there is no pressure on us. Responsibility is the ability to respond. Response may be no less instantaneous than reaction, but it comes from the moment, not the past.

The other major difference between reaction and response is that in reacting we have no choice. Reaction is a surrender of choice. Responding is choosing. We are in control and we respond, or we are out of control and we react. It is our love that responds, our fear that reacts.

25

(Response is generally positive, reaction negative.) To respond is simple, and immensely powerful.

Let me share a couple of incidents from my own life that taught me about the power of response.

Treenie and I once farmed in Tasmania, a small island state off the southern coast of Australia. We lived in the foothills of a mountain for a decade, farming dairy and beef. When we first moved onto the farm, we quickly made friends with our neighbors — all except one couple, Sid and Peg, who never would be friendly.

We had only been on the farm a few months when one of their sons came asking for help, explaining that his mother had been thrown off her horse high up on the mountain road. We went to the rescue in our Land Rover, took Peg to the local hospital, left her son to take the horse home, and then fetched Sid from where he worked and took him to the hospital to be with Peg.

Not even this warmed them to us. Six months later, when a number of our cows found a gap in the fence between Sid's farm and ours, he impounded them! It cost us a lot of money to get them back.

At first, I was all reaction. I cursed and swore revenge. In those days, I weighed over two hundred pounds and was very strong, plus I had a fair skill at judo and boxing, so beating the hell out of Sid was high on my list of priorities. But I never did. I was too civilized. Besides, Treenie wouldn't let me.

Over the next few years Sid accused me of moving a boundary fence in my favor, and of diverting a creek to my property from his. In fact, the fence proved to favor

Sid by eighteen inches, and I found a dam on his side of the creek that obstructed the original bed. This was easily rectified, and even more easily proved.

These and other incidents caused me to realize that Sid truly hated me. Why, I had no clue, but faced with and persecuted by such sheer spite, I began to see beyond it. My reaction ebbed away, and I began to respond to the situation with a tolerant sympathy.

I am not a vindictive person. I do not bear or carry grudges easily, so as soon as I quit reacting, I came to a kind of peace with both Sid and his hate.

Then one day when Treenie and I were in our large, beautiful garden with a couple of visiting friends, I noticed Sid, a rifle in his hands, coming toward us. Before Sid reached us, I murmured to Treenie to go phone for the police. Then I moved away from her, holding Sid's attention. Not that I needed to. The gun was pointed directly at me, and Sid was so focused in hate and rage I doubt he saw anybody else. Our two visitors were both pale faced and anxious. Not quite your usual Sunday afternoon entertainment!

I asked Sid what it was all about, trying to keep his attention on me and to keep him talking. He fairly spit his words, accusing me of stealing his six-thousand-dollar bull, his knuckles white on the gun. In all truth, I felt only mildly alarmed. It did not register that I could lose my life. I felt in complete control, which, given the physical evidence, was stupid.

I managed to keep him talking until the police arrived. When they did come, he welcomed them, for from his distortion of hate, I was the guilty party. I can still remember the shock on his face when they led him away.

Later, the police were annoyed with me because I refused to press charges. I thought Sid needed help, not prosecution, and he did end up in a mental hospital.

Oh, a few incidentals: The bull turned out to be a borrowed, six-hundred-dollar bull, and the gun was loaded. One of the psychologists who worked on Sid's case told me that in all his experience he had never seen such a psychotic hate as Sid held for me. When I asked why, he told me that it was because I am a Pomme! Sid hated the English or—to be more accurate—my being English was the excuse Sid used to express his hate. Sid reacted to me, despite the fact we seldom met, because his life was one of fear-based reaction, not the response of love. Fear-based reaction leads us to be victims, or to look for one. Either way, *we* are the victims.

❧   ❧   ❧

Personal freedom requires that we grow with the years. Do you remember the games we played as children? Do you remember how we sulked over minor things? I well remember that if one of my playmates stopped liking me, then I, naturally, would not like him or her. We would each have a good sulk. Don't laugh—many adults have never grown out of it! Gaining personal freedom means transcending these juvenile games. It means quitting the reactive programs set into place in our youth, and responding to the impact of the moment.

Treenie and I lived in a commune for four years. I could say a lot about that, but for now I will relate a single story.

Anybody who knows anything at all about communes knows that the members' predominant occupation is sitting around in one meeting after another. We could spend two days debating whether lettuce should be grown in straight rows or in circles. It was not a good way to grow vegetables, but a great way to grow people—personal growth under hothouse conditions.

Bruce was one of our older members, another Aries. No matter what I suggested, he would argue against it. Two-day debates were easy when he and I were involved. During one of these sessions, I noticed that no matter what I said, however ridiculous, Bruce would react to counter it. So I began a mischievous game, making increasingly outrageous suggestions, while poor Bruce got more and more steamed up.

Then something unforeseen happened. Quite suddenly, I saw Bruce in a different light. I saw and recognized his courage. In those days I was inclined to steamroll people in communal meetings, and I suddenly recognized that Bruce was always trying to buffer my impact. He cared as much about the community as I did. With a sense of shock, I saw that I respected and admired him for this.

From then on, my previous cool reserve turned to cordiality whenever I met him.

But the change and recognition was only on my side. It did not automatically cause Bruce to like and accept me. He maintained his distance, clearly broadcasting disapproval.

For the first time I was able to leave behind my child-based program, a program of mindless reaction: I don't like you because you don't like me. I was now able to respond, and it felt great! I now liked Bruce, even if he didn't accept me. I discovered a freedom in that. A freedom simple yet powerful enough to completely change my behavior pattern and eventually change his. Ultimately, we became friends.

6

The Two-by-Four Approach

With my wife, Treenie, figuring so strongly in my life, it is natural she be a featured character in this book. To be honest, after thirty-two years of marriage, I am now more of a we than an I!

Treenie is a wonderful person with whom to share life, a woman of insight and great wisdom. However, like all of us, many of her admirable qualities have had to be developed.

Treenie is a very strong person, quiet but strong. Her natural warmth and sincerity tend to hide the strength of her character, yet strength also has to be tempered— frequently by fire. Strength that is rigid may contain structural flaws. Its rigidity is a flaw. This was something that Treenie had to learn, and because of her strength, the lesson required a high-impact approach. As always, when we need to move beyond a self-imposed restriction, life provides the perfect opportunity.

It all began when I invited a new friend, Jack, and his wife, Helen, to dinner one evening. Jack was considerably older than I, and as director of his own company and board member of seven other companies, he was a man of great insight with a wealth of experience. He was also a successful novelist. We met when he invited me, in my capacity as a consultant for organic farming, to advise him on the organic culture of his few acres of Pinot Noir grapes. He not only enjoyed drinking a fine wine, he also wanted to experiment with producing it.

We talked and found we had a lot in common, hence the invitation. This was in the early years of my own writing, and Jack, with forty years experience behind him, became something of a mentor for my literary efforts. He loved writing and the well-crafted word, so when he criticized my written words, I paid careful attention. Jack was a very straight talker—no bullshit!

One evening, I arrived home from a half day with Jack and told Treenie that I had invited them to dinner. She gave me a level stare. "I thought you told me that Helen is a heavy smoker."

"Yes," I said. "So what?"

"Have you forgotten our no-smoking-in-the-house rule?"

I looked at her appealingly. "No, I haven't forgotten, but Helen is a compulsive smoker. We can't tell her not to smoke. It would be impossible for her."

Treenie regarded me unflinchingly. "You know our rule."

"Surely we can flex it a little," I pleaded.

"Definitely not. What's the point of making a no-smoking rule and then bending it for people who smoke? That defeats the whole purpose of the rule."

"I agree with what you're saying in principle, but surely people are more important than rules," I replied.

Treenie stared at me uncompromisingly.

"How about we make an exception for Helen but not for anybody else," I suggested hopefully.

Treenie's words were flat and final. "Absolutely not.

Nobody is smoking in our house."

"So what do I do?" I asked her.

"You will have to phone Jack and tell him."

"If I do, then it will be the end of our dinner date. I know Jack."

"You will be able to work something out."

"Please change your mind," I begged.

Treenie was unyielding. "A rule is a rule."

Reluctantly, I headed for the phone, dialing with fingers suddenly thick and clumsy. Jack answered. I felt acutely embarrassed explaining the situation. I told him no smoking was our rule, not wishing to blame Treenie. He heard me out without interruption as I blundered through my explanation.

"That's okay, Michael," he said with finality. "We won't be coming, that's all. I don't need to embarrass my wife. If she can't be accepted the way she is, we will do better to keep away." The phone clicked in my ear.

I groaned. It was even worse than I had expected. Numb, I walked into the living room to Treenie.

"So what's happening?" she asked brightly.

"They are not coming," I replied stiffly. "That's what's happening. I told you. I hope you're satisfied. Jack did just what I would have done if someone didn't want you with your particular habits."

I slumped in my chair, my expression bleak. For the first time, it dawned on Treenie the position she had forced me into. Not wishing to hurt me, she relented.

"I'm really sorry," she said. "I didn't think it would come to this. I'll accept it if Helen smokes, really. Phone Jack and tell him it's all right."

On a fresh surge of hope, yet filled with an ominous misgiving, I went back to the phone, dialed Jack, and told him our decision.

"That's nice of you, Michael, but under the circumstances it would be very difficult. Helen smokes, and you don't like it—that's not fair to either you or Helen. No, we won't come, but don't worry about it. This won't spoil our friendship." A few more words as it all slipped away from me, our relationship running down the gurgler, and I held a dead phone.

Defeated, I told Treenie what had taken place. Gone now were all traces of the flippancy that had marked her manner and approach to the problem. She looked at me, saw my disappointment and defeat, and it finally hit her. She, who normally encouraged her rather sensitive husband, had ruined a valuable friendship before it ever really got started.

After a long, strained, helpless silence, she began to cry, quietly at first, then with huge, shuddering sobs. "It's all my fault. I was so damned inflexible and now it's too late. I know how much you respect Jack and value his friendship, and now I've ruined it for you. I'm so sorry."

To be truthful, I let her cry. I figured she had earned it.

Next morning, a repentant Treenie suggested we both go see Jack and talk it out. She had never met him and wanted my support for her confessional.

"No," I said. "This was your doing. Besides, knowing what I know of Jack, it wouldn't work. He and I would smooth it over, but he wouldn't have any respect for you and that would be wrong. I don't want his friendship at that cost.

Okay, you made an error and you know it, but you are a person very worthy of respect. I think you should go alone."

Without another word, she got in our car and drove away.

Jack told me what happened next.

Treenie arrived at their home, introduced herself to him and Helen and told them it was she, not I, who had insisted on the no-smoking rule. "I realized too late that friendship is far more important than rules, and that people really matter," she said, and then she broke down and cried. "I knew all that," she sobbed. "I just can't understand how I became so damned rigid and unyielding."

Jack put an arm around her, soothing her, while Helen put the kettle on for the universal balm—a cup of tea.

"Anybody who has the guts to come to this old lion in his own den and be as honest as you doesn't have any real problem," he rumbled. "We all make mistakes once in a while. You've got my respect and," he winked at her, "we *will* come to dinner."

They did, and Helen did not smoke once.

Treenie and I call his the two-by-four method of learning. By that, we mean that whenever we become rigid and inflexible, or unseeing and unyielding, it seems as though life organizes a situation that hits us with enough force to break through our rigidity or our shell of indifference or complacency, or even our habits.

One other thing. The power of impact from a metaphoric length of two-by-four is always in direct proportion to the density of the object to be clobbered!

Simple, huh?

7

Very Effectively Gagged

Have you ever noticed how *things* happen to us in daily life in direct accordance with the way we perceive ourselves? Think about it. I mean that if we do something to someone else that we feel badly about, or regret, invariably something equally unpleasant happens to us. The only trouble is, by the time something happens to us we have already dismissed or forgotten the causative factor.

Treenie and I became familiar with this foible of human behavior when, just over a decade ago, we were involved in the formation and establishment of a commune. The Homeland commune was an experiment in holistic living, consciously combining body, mind, and spirit in our everyday work—or trying to! The four years that Treenie and I lived there was a time of intense personal growth.

You would think that a community of people from all walks of life, living in a lush, subtropical valley, growing our food organically, would be the very epitome of good health. Nothing could be farther from the truth. We were, in fact, growing people—a process we resisted with all the normal perversity available to us, even though growth was the whole purpose of the exercise. You know how it goes: Just because I know it's good for me doesn't mean I won't resist like hell!

So, in direct proportion to our resistance of the personal

growth process, we got sick. I can write about it easily in retrospect, but at the time I suffered with everyone else. We got colds, flu, cuts and sprains, and nasty, nasty tropical ulcers. And we endured a few items such as depression, panic attacks, and feelings of total isolation — total isolation in a commune! All in all, a mixed bag of miseries.

Homeland was open to visitors, and even had a guest program for those who might wish to come and suffer with us for a week or so. A program, I might add, that was constantly filled. I now have a sneaky suspicion that some of our guests came to spend a week just to reinforce how well off they were prior to their visit. But we had fun as well, and sometimes the love was almost tangible.

One man who lived in the area often called in to spend an hour or so with anyone who would chat with him. Allen was a particular thorn in my side. Every time he opened his mouth it seemed to be to criticize or ridicule — and I was very protective of our community. One hot, sunny afternoon when a mild, flulike epidemic had laid many of us low, and we were all commiserating under the shade of our huge Port Jackson fig tree, Allen just happened to drop in.

"It's all in the mind," he told us with a contemptuous glance across our smitten ranks. "If your minds were clear and uncluttered, then your bodies would reflect it. You all need to get your acts together."

I had an overwhelming urge to stuff his mouth with fig leaves, but I sat silently, seething. In retrospect, I guess even that was growth.

Months passed, and one morning I noticed Treenie under

the same user-friendly tree, treating someone for tropical ulcers. I walked over to investigate, and what do you think? It was our visiting smarty-pants, Allen, sick with a bad case of tropical ulcers.

Did I feel concern or compassion? No. I looked him over, sneered, and said, "Don't worry, it's all in your mind. If your mind were clear and uncluttered, your body would reflect it." (I wasn't always the nice guy that people love and admire today.)

Treenie glared at me. "If you can't help us, Michael, go away and leave us in peace."

It was her classic, full-frosted glare, so I knew it was time to clear off, but I walked away deliberately laughing at him.

Deep—way down deep—inside, my conscience stirred. *You'll be sorry*, it called softly, before I shoved it even deeper into unreachable depths.

As I passed the shed that housed our communal tractor, a voice called out, "Hey Michael, I can't get any diesel fuel through this line." I walked over, immediately involved and intrigued.

The fuel line on the tractor was blocked. Being fairly experienced in such things, I put my mouth over one end of the dismantled fuel line and cautiously sucked on it. Without warning, my mouth was instantly flooded. I spat and gagged my way to the nearest washbasin, where I washed out my mouth with soap and water.

And then it hit me. In a flash, I saw the connection between my foul mouthing Treenie's suffering patient and having my mouth filled with foul fuel. It was *you'll-be-sorry* time!

Ever able to acknowledge my faults when life reveals them so scathingly, I walked back down to the tree and into Treenie's don't-you-dare glare.

"I want to apologize for the way I spoke to you," I said. Both patient and Treenie stared at me in astonishment. "My behavior was boorish and offensive," I continued. "I deserve to have my mouth washed out with soap and water for what I said. I'm sorry."

When Allen and Treenie had recovered from the shock of such an abrupt turnaround, we sat and talked. Funny that! Once I got to know Allen, he was a really nice guy. A bit direct and outspoken maybe, but then perhaps I was just a teeny-weeny bit that way myself.

The lesson was very direct and simple—life is like that—and sometimes the lesson is experienced far more harshly than as a mere mouthwash.

On our daughter Tracy's sixteenth birthday, she had a couple of friends over for the day. I was in our living room reading in a large, comfortable chair, when Tracy accidentally trod on my right foot, very painfully wrenching the big toe sideways. If she had been alone, she would have cuddled and fussed over me, making sure I knew how sorry she was. But because her friends were with her, she gave me a curt, embarrassed "Sorry," and left the room.

Not long afterward, one of her friends came rushing in to say that Tracy had cut herself badly. They had been barefoot, and Tracy had stepped on a sliver of glass. When we got to her, she was bleeding profusely. The cut was on her right foot, quite close to the big toe.

We had to take her to hospital and have the foot stitched

up, but it healed just fine. Later, when I talked to Tracy about it, suggesting that it might have been a form of self-inflicted punishment, she looked thoughtful. "You could be right," she said. "When I went outside, I felt really bad about your toe."

All too simple, you think? Observe your own behavior and your family's. You may be in for a surprise.

8
G'Day, Isn't It?

Rain was gushing along the streets in drenching squalls one cold, windy, midwinter day in Melbourne, Oz, as Treenie and I dashed in through the door of a small, cozy health-food shop.

The girl behind the counter smiled a forced smile at us, her face a bit pinched, her energy down. "Isn't it an absolutely awful day," she commented.

"No," I replied. "It's a beautiful day."

She looked at me in surprise, not sure she had heard me correctly. "But it's cold out there, and pouring with rain, and there's a gale blowing."

"Yes," I replied, "that's all correct, but that's the weather you're describing. The weather is not the day. Suppose you had a week's holiday at home and you were reading a great book, curled up snug and warm by a fire. What difference would the weather make to your day then? None at all. Yet here you are in a cozy shop, warm and dry, and you call it an awful day. Do you know what that does to you?"

"No," she said, looking unsure.

"It puts you at the mercy of how you set up your day, that's what it does. The way you say it is becomes the way it is.

"What if you had jumped out of bed this morning saying, 'Wow, what a wonderful day to be alive! I know I'm

43

going to have a great day today!' And when you looked out the window, you had said, 'The weather is rotten, but the day is great!' You would have been open to having a wonderful day. Your day could be positive and uplifting despite the weather."

I gave her a big, warm smile. "Here we are, having a wonderful discussion about life, which has caused you to shift from looking miserable when we came in, to cheerful and smiling—and it's still raining and windy."

The shop girl was smiling openly now. "I'm trying to decide if you're for real, or not." She looked at Treenie. "Is he always like this?" she asked.

"I'm afraid so," Treenie replied cheerfully.

The girl looked thoughtful. "You know," she said, "I've never looked at it like that before. I really think you are right." Suddenly, she looked delighted. "What a novel idea. That's the way I'm going to do it from now on."

You get the idea? Simple, isn't it?

9
The Hair-Shirt Belief

There are some commonly held, extremely powerful beliefs that can be very unpleasant, even hazardous. To make the situation even trickier, some of these beliefs to which we unwittingly adhere are subconscious. We are not even aware we believe what we believe! I once believed that humans grow through suffering. Although I did not realize it, way down in my subconscious there was a program that said we are born in sin and we are cleansed through suffering; just as physical muscles grow by lifting heavy weights, so spiritual muscles grow by overcoming the burden of suffering.

I now consider this a particularly nasty belief, albeit a very common one. Naturally enough, such a belief manifests in suffering. The irony is, we often do grow as a result of suffering, which strengthens and maintains the belief.

Fortunately, we can change the inner program. Let me share my own story of inner change with you.

When I was twenty-nine, I ruptured a disk in my lower spine. Opportunities abound for such a thing when you are a farmer. A visit to the doctor was little help. "You've strained a muscle," he said, dismissing me. "Take a few of these little red pills to ease the pain and you'll soon be fit again."

He was wrong. Seven years later, after many bouts of

intense and crippling pain, a different doctor examined my X rays and pronounced the injury a ruptured disk, now a chronic, compounded problem that could lead to eventual disability.

This is where I have to take full responsibility for my own pain. In my midthirties, I became totally committed to personal and spiritual growth. Thus, my inner commitment to growth triggered my subconscious belief—I created pain so I could grow through suffering. I not only manifested the back injury, but also took myself to an incompetent doctor so the injury could become chronic. Never underestimate the creative power we each contain! The art of living is to use that power in a more aware and loving way.

For twenty years, I used the pain in my lower back to create the suffering I subconsciusly believed I needed for inner growth. At one stage, the pain caused most of the muscles in my body to spasm, curling me into a tight fetal position on the floor in the living room. Eventually, when my bladder was full, I was shocked to find I could not pass any urine. The pain in my back was so intense, I could not get a message to my bladder to release. Hours later, I was turning yellow as my body attempted to reabsorb the urine. Next thing I knew, I was hospitalized, catheterized, in traction, and drugged.

Four years later, still without a clue that my pain was self-induced, there came another dramatic confrontation with suffering. But this was even more creative.

Early one morning, having bounced out of bed with my usual Aries vigor, I was standing in the shower, well soaped, water cascading over my head and shoulders, when a strange feeling came over me. Despite the hot water, I felt as though ice were trickling down my spine. In the hot, steamy enclosure of the shower cubicle, I felt a ribbon of arctic cold. It was not a coldness of the skin, but of the inner self.

Even as I struggled to understand what was happening, an overwhelming sense of blessedness seemed to fill the cold space. I knew that if I could shift my sense of identity away from my physical body and become open and receptive, then I could become one with this intangible benediction, this exaltation hovering just a hair's breadth away.

Mixed feelings of jubilation and despair surged through me. I was so close to a source of transcendent love, yet so far away. I felt as if some powerful light were waiting for a fusion of our energies; but sadly, it remained beyond me. It was love as a distant echo, rather than the overwhelming experience. It faded swiftly, jubilation receded, despair remained.

I had failed, I realized, because I had tried to grab hold of the experience. I had always believed that my greatest gift in life was my simplicity, but I was not simple enough to simply let go.

Afterward, I went outside to feed our dozen hens. Five minutes later, as I watched them pecking at their morning feed, my mind on the shower experience, my lower back suddenly and dramatically went into violent spasm.

I collapsed as though shot.

I lay still. With my history of back pain, I knew the score.

47

After a while, as the spasms eased, I attempted a shout. Within moments, Treenie and Tracy appeared.

Best to draw a curtain across the next hour or so—it was painful—and resume at my close friend John Caporale's chiropractic clinic. Supported by his strong arms, I staggered into his treatment room and onto the padded adjustment table. For twenty minutes, I lay under a heat lamp designed to soften me up, then I had a spell of massage to relax the rigid muscles. Next, John attempted to maneuver me into position for an adjustment, but perversely, the pain flared again and I could not take it. Undaunted, he set me up for a half hour of mild electrical impulse treatment—and I got worse. Finally, I ended up curled in a fetal position on John's carpeted floor, seized in the clamp of another violent muscle spasm.

I felt the most terrible despair. I felt myself giving in, surrendering to the pain. I felt that if it consumed me, it would no longer matter. I had never felt this way before. Always I had resisted the pain with all my might, but I could no longer do so. I seemed to float in pain, yet incredibly, once again that benediction of love and light arose and hovered close by me.

I knew beyond all doubt that if I could totally surrender my pain and "myself," then I and the fullness of love would become united. With this knowledge came an awareness that the pain was in my body, and I could surrender my pain. But "my self" exists on another plane and, sadly, I knew it was impossible to surrender that.

As I let go of the pain in a way that had never before been possible, the benediction of love fused with me. But it was only a partial fusion, and only my physical pain was affected. Even so, the pain became no more than a distant, background murmur, and I was able to get up from the floor.

I would like to be able to say that I now realized that I was the author of my pain, but my knowledge had not yet encompassed this truth. By the end of that day, my euphoria was fading and the pain was intensifying. However, I had no more searing spasms; the pain was now deep and constant.

Under John's care, I gradually improved over the next few weeks, until I was once more reasonably free from pain. Just when I could safely say I was better, my oldest son, Duncan, came to spend a couple of days with us.

Without going into details, I must say that he and I had a huge row. Duncan is very volatile, very articulate, and very powerful. He had long contained an enormous amount of rage, dating back to his childhood, so when it all came to a head, it just exploded out of him. Probably for the first time in my life, I became vulnerable to another person's anger. I attempted to block him out mentally, but something inside of me would not allow that to happen. Duncan maintained his rage in an outpouring of verbal abuse and accusations for over an hour, unaware of and unconcerned about what was happening to me.

When he got up and walked out of the room, he left behind a shattered husk. I, who was used to annihilating others in any verbal clash, had been devastated. I felt as though a flame gun had been applied to my psyche, cauterizing all feeling. For the rest of that afternoon, I experienced an inner hurt unlike anything I had known before.

Rather than easing, the hurt grew as the hours passed. I lay in bed awake all that night, oblivious to Treenie's words of comfort, and the pain grew.

Next morning, I forced myself with a real effort to eat some breakfast on the front veranda. I was totally unprepared for the Duncan who met me there, full of good cheer, asking how I was feeling.

"I think you had better go home," I said stiffly.

With the words hardly out of my mouth, Duncan exploded once more into a fury of offended outrage. Within minutes, he was throwing clothes into his suitcase and shouting at the rest of the household. I retreated to the bedroom to nurse my shattered psyche. Bedlam raged. Everyone shouted at everyone—all except me. I lay on the bed, feeling sorry for myself.

Treenie suddenly burst into the bedroom. "Michael, you must come and talk this out with Duncan. You can't let the family break up like this. Don't you see? This is another test." And with those words Treenie stormed out of the room.

I lay silently. Ever since I had made my commitment to inner growth, I had indeed faced one test after another. Reluctantly, I saw that this was another one. A damned sneaky one. And one I had almost failed. Insight came with flashlight clarity. Duncan had been the catalyst for my pain, but somewhere in the process I had become consumed by overpowering self-pity.

At the moment of insight, that benediction of love hovered close by once again. I knew that to become united with this higher love I had to surrender my pain. But how? This was not pain in my body; this pain was me—I *was* the pain.

I had no idea how to let go of this inner hurt. All my years of personal growth seemed of little value when I faced a moment of truth. Consequently, the surrender of my hurt was not much more than a token gesture, but it was the best I could manage. It was enough that I was able to get up from my bed, walk out into the living room, put my arms around Duncan, and tell him I loved him. And I meant it. I knew, without any real understanding of how I knew it, that as a catalyst Duncan was offering me a great gift.

Later, as he and I sat on the lawn talking, he said a strange thing: "This has been a real catharsis for me, and an ending; but it's a beginning for you."

"What do you mean?" I asked.

"I don't know," he said.

Moments later, Treenie called out to say that Tracy was missing. In all the turmoil of our big row, she had vanished, and was unaware of the happy ending.

I knew intuitively where she was, and went bounding down the steep steps leading to the river that flowed past our house. Sure enough, I found Tracy sitting on my favorite river rock, crying.

We cuddled, and went back up the twenty or so steps, taking our time. But for me, the damage was done. Bounding down the steps had thrown my back into total disarray. When Duncan left at the end of that day, I was flat on my back once again.

For the next six weeks, although John worked on me, I made little progress. I could walk, but only in a painful shuffle.

During this time, an old friend visited us for a couple of days. We had known her when we lived in Tasmania; she had been an important influence on our lives. Although a strong friendship remained, the visit showed how far apart our philosophies had grown. When she left, her parting remark was "It's been lovely seeing you again Michael, but are you aware that you have lost your joy?"

With that, and a kiss and farewell for Treenie, she departed.

That's fine for you to say, I thought bitterly, as her plane climbed into the blue sky. You would loose your joy, too, if you were suffering as much as I am. But the remark haunted me.

John worked on me twice a day sometimes, and I could sense his growing frustration with my failure to respond. Five weeks passed. One Sunday after another treatment, he told me that my back was so unresponsive he was not sure whether he was doing me any good, and he questioned whether we should continue treatment. The implications frightened me. That evening, pain again crawled and cramped its fingers across my lower back and buttocks. Why didn't I respond to treatment? Would I become a hospital case again? Could I end up crippled? Pain is very tiring, however; finally, I slept.

Sunlight awakened me. I opened my eyes, only to squeeze them shut in anguish.

I was having an attack of cellulitis. Distressing more than

painful, cellulitis is the inflammation of the subcutaneous tissue of the face. It had bothered me for about five years and although I knew it was stress related, nothing I tried seemed to prevent it. Symptoms were sensitivity to light, and swelling around my eyes, in the jaw, ears, nose, and mouth—all with extreme itching.

I had cellulitis again, and I could hardly move with lower back pain. Then, amazingly, from within the dark depths of despair came a light of brilliant intensity, flooding me with revelation. It was as though I saw myself clearly, all crap put aside.

This was it—crunch time! For most of my life, I had taken my body to doctors to heal, and ultimately they could not heal me. Next, thinking it more enlightened, I took my body to chiropractors and naturopaths to heal, and, again, they could not help me. I *knew* now that it was time for me to take full responsibility for my health. I knew now that ultimately no one else could. Although I had no idea how to go about it, I knew I could do it.

I told Treenie. I got her to promise that no matter what developed—this was it! Even if the cellulitis threatened my life, so be it. This was to be a final confrontation.

Please understand that I was not trying to be dramatic. I *knew* that if I could not follow this through, I would continue to suffer for the rest of my life.

No dramatic healing followed this revelation. Another two days of pain and misery passed, yet my inner knowing that I had the ability to heal myself grew even stronger. Most of the time I was confined to bed, but on the third day, making a determined effort, I managed to stagger out onto the veranda. I was sitting in extreme discomfort on an old sofa, when Yvonne, a friend, called in for a chat.

"My God! You look rough, Michael."

Not exactly words of comfort. I told her that despite appearances, I was healing myself. Yvonne raised her eyebrows, but said nothing.

A few minutes later, Treenie appeared with a tray of coffee. It was obvious she had heard our exchange.

"Michael believes we grow through suffering," she said, "but I don't accept that. I believe we grow through love. We don't have to suffer. Michael is attached to wearing a hair shirt."

How many times had I heard her make the same remark about my suffering? Now, for the first time, a ring of truth from her words echoed in my head. Had I been attached to suffering all these years? Under the echo of Treenie's words, there came another echo: *Michael, do you realize you have lost your joy?*

Oh my God! I had not lost my joy—I had never really had it. I had been happy, especially in my marriage to Treenie, very happy, but joy, real joy? A joy that spoke of peace, living without fear, living by grace? No, I had never experienced it. How could I? How could I have joy if I believed I could only grow through suffering?

It was my moment of truth. The lie of my belief stood exposed.

For a moment, I faltered. What do I do now? As soon as I posed the question to myself, I was gripped by a fierce desire to face myself. To look into a mirror and see me, my self-deceit, my pain, and my suffering, and maybe find the slightest trace of joy. I desperately wanted to be able to tell myself that I loved myself. And even more, I wanted to be able to hear it!

Struggling to my feet, I lurched my painful way from the veranda into my youngest son Russell's room. A Leo, he had a large preening mirror propped on the floor. With my eyes closed, I slumped to the floor in front of the mirror and, with a surge of hope, opened them.

I recoiled in shock. The face that stared back at me had four days' growth of beard and was grotesquely swollen with cellulitis. Heavy bags hung under eyes filled with pain; my left ear resembled a raw steak slapped carelessly on the side of my head. My jaw hung in a swollen fold, and bright red inflammation quilted my face in a random pattern. It was a face of suffering, and in this moment's truth, I knew that it was my creation, the manifestion of a belief. If there is suffering, then this was it.

Speechless, I stared at this human travesty, while tears trickled unbidden down my cheeks, I felt I had reached the bottom. I was ready for my life to end. For all those years of suffering, I had been searching for Self, to know who I am, for self-realization, and that search had reduced me to this — abject failure.

Deep inside, I surrendered myself — totally. I did not give up; I gave in. I surrendered my belief in suffering, my physical pain, my search for Self. I surrendered my knowledge, my self-righteousness, and all the belief systems by which I had so long been bound. In that moment, I let go of everything that kept me from joy, from living by grace, from experiencing *real* peace. I even surrendered my life. And then the strangest thing happened. As I watched a tear drip from the end of my nose, an old, long-forgotten memory came tumbling back.

In England as a child, I used to hate the way a cold winter day caused adults' noses to drip. In our cold classrooms, one particular teacher always had a drip hanging from her nostrils; it made me writhe with revulsion. Now, I gazed at the drip hanging from my own nose—and began to giggle! Simultaneously, the fullness of love and benediction was once again with me, but this time my surrender was complete. The little "i" had momentarily died in the completeness of my surrender, to be reborn as I at one with the fullness of love. With this rebirth came the exaltation of knowing who I am.

Beyond this, I will not try to recapture the experience in words, which are inadequate. Suffice it to say that the experience transformed me and my life. Within thirty minutes, all trace of cellulitis had disappeared, not to return. And twenty years of back pain came to an end.

As I write this, five years have passed, and the pain has not recurred. Nor has my belief in suffering.

Because I surrendered a belief based in pain and suffering, and made the switch from despair to joy, I know you can, too. This does not require a higher education, or a superior IQ, or a Ph.D. in theology.

This only requires the courage to choose love, that greatest of all powers that allows you to be who you are as life weaves its wondrous changes in you, and the commitment to stay with it, no matter what. It's simple—not easy—but powerful beyond imagining.

10

A Time to Quit

What is more elusive than inner peace? This is a nice subject to think about because it is something we all need. You will realize from these pages that the experiences described here are random slices of my life. Peace was not always my companion.

I have met, and continue to meet, people who seek inner peace while harboring hostility toward the world in general, surely a futile way to find what they look for. During my four years at the Homeland commune, I learned that peace cannot be cajoled, pursued, or manipulated. Like so many others, I pursued it as though it were something outside of me, something that might be found under rainbows or in tranquil rivers. However, my experiences at Homeland gave me an intellectual understanding of peace, in spite of myself. I had yet to learn that peace is not intellectual—that peace is an experience, not an understanding.

We had many visitors at Homeland. Some, no doubt, were attracted by the diversity and stimulation of a bunch of human misfits, some by their own inner seeking, and yet others by the sheer physical beauty of the place. We had about 345 acres of green hills, eucalyptus forests, open fields, and a river. And what a river! It bordered our land all along one side of the property, creating a natural division between us and the lush rain forest that clambered up the escarpment to a plateau far above. Crystal clear, the river flowed over a bed of water-polished stones, only to sink, sighing, into a deep pool to contemplate the ocean. I loved that river. I still do.

Just as the river attracted me, so also many Homeland guests fell under its spell. One was a middle-aged, dark-haired, very serious guy named Ben, who spent most of each day down by the river, away from all communal activities, including the guest program. I had little to do with him, but we got into conversation one sunny morning as we shared the tenuous shade of a thin-needled river pine. For a while, we watched river mullet leaping in a silver flashing arc from the water's surface.

"I've heard that you come here to avoid communal chores," I said mildly. Nothing like a challenge to get things off to a good start!

Ben looked worried, but he always looked worried. "I know that," he said. "It isn't true."

I waited, but nothing more was forthcoming. "So apart from the obvious beauty of the river—which we all enjoy—what keeps you here nearly all day?"

"I'm here to find peace." He spoke with a reserved dignity.

"Aren't we all," I replied with a touch of cynicism. "Anyway, how can the river give you peace? I understand peace as an inner quality expressing out, rather than an outer something that can be drawn in."

"Oh, no! You're wrong," he burst out. "If I sit here long enough, I can soak up the peace of the river and nurture it within me."

"Like bread soaking up gravy?"

He looked pained. "It's a mad place where I live in the city. Endless lines of noisy, stinking traffic and an endless, mindless rush day after day, month after month. This river is the opposite of everything I experience in my everyday life. This *is* peace."

He was quiet for a while, and I said nothing. I felt I had already said enough.

"So I just soak it up," he continued determinedly, "and I feel at peace." He gave me a challenging look, daring me to defy either his logic or his feelings.

"What happens when you go back to the city?" I asked. "How long does this river peace last?"

"For as long as I can hang onto it. I remember the river long after I leave. I hold it in my mind's eye and I concentrate on it. In this way, I can shut out the city."

I saw regret in his dark brown eyes, and I knew despite his words that his peace was an unsatisfactory illusion. "And you think this is inner peace?" I asked gently.

"It's the best I can manage," he said, the dignity back in his voice. "It's easy enough for you to talk about. You live here, not in the city with its pressures. You can soak up as much of the river as you like. I've watched you. You swim in it and you meditate by it. You can't tell me that it doesn't give you peace."

If only peace were that easy, I thought. But I said nothing for a while, just staring at the river as it flowed past us. I felt a surge of compassion for this very serious man who just wanted to be at peace with himself and the world.

When I spoke, my words were reflective. "I've lived in

this community nearly four years. Like you, I once believed that the river offered peace, while the diversity of the people who live here—some of whom I don't even like—offered a great deal of confusion and discord. Of course, there's been clarity and harmony as well, and friendship with a rare degree of caring. Nevertheless, it has not been easy for me to live here. I doubt that it's easy for anyone. Still, the unavoidable human interaction in a commune has forced me to face a truth—you cannot find peace outside of yourself. Not in rainbows, nor in crystal rivers.

"When you sit by this river, you are overwhelmed by the powerful nature of your environment—and you think this is peace. It is not. When you go back to the city and you are overwhelmed by the noisy harshness of your environment, you think that is your discord. It is not." I paused, allowing him time to digest what I was saying.

"In each case, you become a victim of your environment. You happen to be in harmony with the flow of the river, while the city is stressful. In a different mood, this river could burst its banks and drown you. Where then the peace?" I took a breath and went on. "I have learned that peace is found in the most unexpected places. Or, rather, the most unexpected places enable you to find peace within yourself. I have found more peace in the center of conflict than down by this river."

I laughed at his expression of surprise. "It's all a paradox. If you were to live in a commune of saints, entirely without any personal friction or discord, you would find yourself emulating the saints. But peace would not be your reality; it would be your act. The act of peace is not

60

peace. Peace is not needing the act. In fact, peace is not needing."

I smiled ruefully. "I know all this, but I don't happen to experience very much peace myself. Peace is being able to live with equanimity in conflict, not protecting you from it. You wouldn't believe how many times I've used this river to shelter myself from conflict, but that never has given me peace, just breathing space. Eventually I discovered that by living fully in the commune, being part of its anger, part of its discord, part of its everyday emotional and mental confrontations and interactions—and part of its love—gradually, peace finds me. While I search for peace, it eludes me, but when I live fully in all the conflict there is peace! How's that for a paradox?"

There was a long, comfortable silence.

"I appreciate your honesty," Ben said sincerely. "Obviously, what applies in the commune applies in the city. It doesn't make it any easier, but I get the gist of it. You're saying that if I can find peace in the city, instead of an environmentally induced peace—which is really an illusion—I will find my own inner peace." He grinned. "Or it will find me."

"You've got the idea. It's something to which I'm fully committed. I can't imagine a better purpose in life."

As we walked back to the commune together, Ben had a last grumble. "I really believed the river could give me peace. Now I don't have any justification for spending all my time there. Come to think of it, I won't have any real excuse to run away from the city and its turmoil."

"You can always run *to* the river, rather than away from

the city. There's a vast difference, and the difference is within your sense of self. When you are no longer in conflict with the city, you will have no need to run from it. I believe inner peace to be our natural heritage, not an impossibility," I replied, expressing a far greater wisdom than I felt.

11

Father, Dear Father

People can expend a huge amount of energy that we dearly need for everyday life on resentment. Quite often what we resent is, in fact, of great benefit to us. Resentment is the blind focus of very negative emotions. It is one-eyed, seeing no more than a single, resented aspect of an event or individual.

In Treenie's case, resentment was directed toward a person, her father. This is her story in her own words:

"As the firstborn in my family, I must have been rather a disappointment to my father, because, like most farmers, he wanted a son to help with all the hard work. Consequently, I grew up with a deep subconscious need of his approval. To please him, I worked far harder than was necessary, and for longer hours. Pleasing him was paramount in my life.

"Even though I enjoyed going to school when I was young, my father frequently kept me at home to work on the farm. I remember one term when I attended only two weeks of school. My teacher's remarks on my school report reflected this: 'Treenie could do better if she attended school regularly.'

"My father was very strict, and I was always looking for crumbs of acknowledgment and appreciation, but I did not receive much. At fifteen years of age, when I left school, I was told that I was not clever enough for anything else but working on the farm. I can only assume that this judgment was based on my school report. It was definitely a no-win situation. And when my father made it clear that he had kept me until now, and now I had to earn my keep, my dreams of becoming a nurse were quickly shattered.

"Despite all this, the one thing I looked forward to was receiving a wage for my work. I can still remember the disappointment I felt when I finished my first week's work and received no money. Each succeeding week was the same. I was mortified. My father did give me some money when I went shopping, but that was very little.

"Because he was so strict, I was not allowed to go dancing or to the cinema with my friends on a Saturday night. That hurt. My only real outlet was playing the organ at the local Methodist Church three times each Sunday.

"Another of my father's rules was no dating until I was twenty-one years old. Can you believe that? However, in the summer of my nineteenth year, surprisingly, he allowed me to go on a church Youth Club holiday. You can imagine how I enjoyed the two-hundred-mile journey to the north of England with a busload of other teenagers. Our destination was a huge, old boarding school, where we stayed for a week in the glorious Yorkshire countryside, close to the coast. Even the weather was perfect.

"The first night, at about one o'clock in the morning, when we finally had quieted down, a thunderous knocking echoed along the corridors. With a great deal of muttering, a couple of the attendant clergy roused themselves to open the huge front door. Most of us stood in giggling clusters along the balcony, looking down into the main entrance hall on two young men. One of them glanced up at us, and his eyes met and held mine. It was Michael! Apparently, his friend had managed to persuade him—despite his dislike of 'namby-pamby church Youth Clubs'—to act as navigator and accompany him on the holiday. With a bit of arm-twisting by his mother, Michael had reluctantly agreed.

"The following morning, we all congregated in the hall to hear the rules governing our stay. Starting the next day, we would be rostered in small groups on a daily basis to do dish washing and other small chores. I did not see Michael that day, but remained with the group I had befriended on the bus.

"On Monday morning, the week's roster was pinned up for all to see. I looked at it curiously. My name had been crossed off the Tuesday roster and written in on Monday. Sid and Roger, from the group I was friendly with, suggested that someone was pulling a stunt. They wanted me with them, the way the roster had previously allocated, but my sense of rightness directed me to accept it as it was.

"Michael and I met that morning over the dishes at the huge kitchen sink. Only later did he confess that it was he who had altered the duty list. He had been there as it was pinned up, and because he was listed for kitchen duty that Monday he had swiftly hatched this scheme to get to know me. I didn't know whether to be angry or flattered, but by then it was too late—we became inseparable, and I knew I loved him.

"My first major confrontation with my father came when

the holiday was over, and he told me I could not see Michael again. I responded that not only would I see Michael, but that he was coming to tea the following Sunday.

"Would you believe Michael cycled forty miles on an old Hercules bicycle to keep that date? When he arrived, my father sulked in his bedroom for three hours, refusing to meet him. When he finally did emerge, bullied and persuaded by my mother, he took to Michael as though he were a long lost son. I have to admit, Michael does have a certain charm!

"I stayed working on my father's farm until Michael and I married three years later. By this time, I had learned to put my mind to whatever job I did. I didn't fight it, however unpleasant the work. I learned to enjoy and really 'be with' what I was doing. I learned that if I applied myself wholeheartedly, then even the most mundane chores could become creative and pleasant.

"In spite of this attitude, my formative years left me with a deep-seated resentment toward my father. I resented him for exploiting me as a person. I resented him for not paying me for my work, thus lowering my own feelings of self-worth. I resented him for never once appreciating all the effort I extended on his behalf—physical effort that sometimes left me weak and shaking at the end of a grueling day's work. I resented that he told me what I was *not* capable of, rather than what I *was*. I still carried the resentment with me when Michael and I emigrated to Australia a few years after we were married. There is irony in the fact that it was my father's indifference toward me that made emigration an easy choice. There is even greater irony in the grieving process he went through when we left, as though I had died. Such was his inability to deal with my departure.

"Michael and I were farming in Tasmania, the island state, and one day when I was washing up at the kitchen sink, looking out over our beautiful farm, I realized that I was very happy with my life and even more happy with who I was. I became aware that I really liked myself, as a person. Then my thoughts turned to my father, and I realized that it was he who had helped make me the person I am today. No matter how inadvertently, he more than anyone had molded me in those early years.

"Suddenly, I felt an overwhelming gratitude to him, followed by a strong, clear surge of insight, and a feeling of something turning right around inside me. I felt elated, as though I had let go of a heavy burden, to be replaced by a feeling of freedom. All resentment for my father ended, never to return."

Treenie had discovered that most simple of truths. When we look within ourselves, or look back over our lives without judgment, what once appeared so bad can take on a whole new meaning. The trick is — without judgment.

12

Signposts to Destiny

D o you notice the signposts in your life? I don't mean those along the roadside, but the far more subtle messages we give ourselves in daily life—messages designed to indicate the way to be, as well as the way to go. Such signposts are easy to ignore because we have little training in the observation or understanding of them.

When Treenie and I first arrived in America to promote my previous book and conduct seminars, we spent a week in Tiburon, California, getting to know our publishers, Hal and Linda Kramer. At their invitation, we accepted an offer to stay for a few weeks at their holiday home in Bolinas, while Treenie organized our impending tour. Michael Kramer, Hal's son, along with his wife, Stacy, and infant, Seph, offered to transport us to Bolinas.

I had decided not to drive while in the United States, for between my amazing ability to get lost and thirty-five years of driving on the left side of the road, I figured it was in our best interest.

On the way, engaged in easy conversation, I watched the picturesque scenery unfold. We passed Stinson Beach, and followed the coast road around the huge saltwater lagoon that marks the approach to Bolinas. Marsh and wading birds clustered there in large, multicolored groups, heads bobbing and wings fluttering, either swimming on the ebb tide, or stalking on stilt legs over muddy flats. To my surprise and delight, a seal lay on the muddy shoreline directly off the road. As we passed, it waved one flipper as though to acknowledge us. Not for one moment am I suggesting that it did, in fact, wave to us. Probably it was shifting its postion and we happened along as the flipper flapped, but it *was* nice timing.

As we reached the unmarked intersection where one turns off to Bolinas, a deer stepped into the road, stopping us and the car in front of us. For a few, brief moments the deer stood undecided, sniffing the air; then lightly it skipped back into the trees.

A little while later, we drove into Bolinas, and another incident occurred. Two men were fighting, or, to be really accurate, a large guy, shouting hysterically, knocked down a much smaller guy. The smaller guy scrambled to his feet and stood his ground, but, wisely, he said nothing, while the big man screamed accusations at him for the next ten minutes. By the time we had purchased a few necessary items such as sticky buns and homemade pizza, the excitement was over, but it left an odd, mildly disturbing impression as we drove up to the house.

Later, when Michael and his family had departed, Treenie and I sat back to talk about the unusual circumstances of our arrival. Treenie was in no doubt: "Nature has welcomed us, but the human message tells us to keep away. I think we are here to be nurtured by Nature, not to be involved with people."

And so it proved to be. Life had offered us a signpost, indicating how to be where we were, and we accepted those terms. The spirit of Bolinas Bay opened its heart to us, and the few people who came into our lives during those precious six weeks were gentle and sensitive. But although we were invited to join various group activities and to become involved in events in Bolinas, we trusted and followed the signposts of life.

Those few weeks were enough to prove the wisdom of our interpretation. It was a time for simplicity, a time to be quiet and *feel* the power of life. We even ignored the television, which sulked in blank silence, unused and unneeded.

❀   ❀   ❀

The Bolinas signposts might fairly be described as subtle, but others in our life have been startlingly obvious.

Many years ago, when I was in my midtwenties, and my father was suffering in the last stages of cancer, he realized it was time for him to make his last will and testament. I'm sure his generation frequently put off making their wills because the action was too close a reminder of death. Whatever the reason, will making was regularly overlooked in previous generations of our family.

One afternoon, the family solicitor, whom Dad had known since his school days, came to visit. They discussed all aspects of the will, ironing out the necessary details. Then the solicitor went back to his office to put it all down on paper for Dad to sign. However, instead, the solicitor went back to his office, had a massive heart attack, and dropped dead.

News of the death distressed Dad, and at this point his own deterioration accelerated; he was unable to muster

71

the required concentration, and the will never got made.

Within a few weeks, he died. Dad had been a farmer, and having worked with him for the previous eleven years, I continued to run the farm, but things were no longer the same. Suffice it to say that within a few months my brother and I agreed to sell the farm, each taking a share and going our separate ways. Treenie and I were going to build a large, modern piggery on a particular piece of land, and plans for that were well under way while the legal aspects of the estate were thrashed out.

Then my brother telephoned: "I've been making a few calculations, Michael," he said, "and it doesn't look so good. I estimate that we'll get about half the money we expected by the time the death duties have been paid." A few more words were spoken but I scarcely heard them. That single sentence had laid to waste a cherished dream. (Thank God!) Half the money we expected fell quite a way short of what our piggery required. Only one reality remained, and I spoke it aloud to Treenie when I walked back into the living room. "Let's emigrate!"

The idea to emigrate had been mentioned a few times, but it never had been considered seriously. Now, however, the signposts were up and they spoke a bold clear message. Our future did not lie in a farming career in England, nor in the pig industry.

Ironically, when our plans to emigrate had been finalized, we discovered that my brother's calculations and his phone call reflected his own worries more than the facts, and we inherited nearly half as much again as previously calculated. To this day, my brother does not know what prompted that fatal phone call that became the deciding factor in our plans.

We all come to crossroads in our life. We all must decide which way to go, and invariably we all have signposts pointing the way to our greatest inner growth potential. Often the scariest direction is the one indicated, a factor that helps blind us to the subtle signposts along our journey.

Of course, sometimes signposts are such obvious inspirations we cannot miss them. Following a visit to our families, Treenie and I flew out of the United Kingdom on our way to the United States. We were still gaining altitude, wisps of cloud hanging around the plane, when Treenie drew my attention to the window. There, in the most glorious technicolor, a shadow of the DC-10 was imprinted on a white cloud, totally encircled by a double rainbow. The rainbow hovered just beyond the wing tip, the shadow plane reduced to about six feet long, while the spectrum of color seemed to enclose it in a cocoon of promise — another signpost. Fanciful? We don't think so. This was our first-ever visit to America, and we had waited a few years to get the timing right. The rainbow confirmed our timing, and the shadow plane in the rainbow indicated that our travels would be blessed. And they were. Rainbows have always been significant in Treenie's and my life, invariably imparting blessings and confirmation.

How easy it is to dismiss the rainbows in our lives as coincidental happenings, freaks of chance and Nature. I do not see life in terms of chance happenings, nor do I see Nature as separate from me. If I did, this book would not be written, for my essential message is that our simplicity sees life without duplicity. Our simplicity touches the essence of life, revealing in its hidden messages the connection of all things. Recognizing the signposts helps to develop our insight, our inner power.

13

A Monarch in Need

I am a lover of Nature. By this I do not mean I give an emotive gush at every bird or flower, or have a fanatical desire to camp out at any opportunity. I simply mean that while I have a great appreciation for a physical nature, I also relate to what I call "the spirit of Nature." My experiences with Nature indicate that beyond the form, there is the formless. It is the mystery of this intangible, metaphysical, yet entirely natural spiritual energy that evokes the greatest response within me.

I have no doubt that we humans dramatically underestimate the intelligence of Nature. We have an arrogance that assumes intelligence to be the ultimate human prize, thus we relate to Nature in a limited fashion. Most people are content to be onlookers of Nature; I try to participate spiritually, with a merging of consciousness. The nice thing about it is that it opens me to the miraculous—where power and simplicity combine.

Most of this book has been written in Queensland, Oz, but while on tour in America I continued to observe and record the simple everyday incidents that so intrigue me.

I did so for a few glorious weeks of spring when Treenie and I lived in our publishers' holiday home in Bolinas, a place so noted for its beauty that the locals refuse any road signs to signify its existence. As fast as a signpost is erected, it is as quickly removed by midnight marauders. Because the tiny town is less than an hour from San Francisco, the locals also fight any signs of building development. Having seen the environmental destruction of progress, I don't blame them.

Each morning while we were there, Treenie and I strolled the few minutes it took to a lookout point complete with a seat, which, situated on the little mesa, overlooks the whole area. Directly opposite, Stinson Beach lies like a narrow golden scarf draped across the bay, its fragile, ocean side pounded with unceasing vigor by the Pacific. Bisected by a single road serving the needs of a couple of rows of sturdy wooden houses, and a few salt-resistant pines, its other, more sheltered shoreline borders a large tranquil lagoon where the seals live. When the tide sweeps in, the lagoon is flooded; when the tide recedes, its huge flats are exposed.

From our lookout, we were a few hundred feet above the gap between Stinson Beach and Bolinas, an area where the tidal flow has created a deep, narrow channel between the open sea and the lagoon. My favorite pastime was to sit for hours watching the seals swim back and forth along the channel. They swam with a lazy grace, indolence in every gesture, fishing and floating on the brisk current. The seal population was somewhere around fifty animals, so despite their many hours basking in the sun on a mud bank, I could generally count on a few being active.

One morning as I reached our usual seat, I noticed a long-haired white cat about a hundred yards off. Sitting down while also reaching out on an inner level, I called,

"Puss, Puss, come on." I was completely unprepared for the result. The cat had been watching me with the nonchalance that only a cat can manage, when suddenly it raced toward me through the long grass, and leaped the last six feet to land with a scramble of fur and claws in my lap.

I was dumbfounded. Immediately, the cat put a large paw up onto each side of my neck, gently engaged the claws far enough to grip my shirt collar, and pulled my head down to stare into my eyes. It regarded me quizzically. I returned the gaze with some bewilderment. This was the most uncatlike behavior I had ever encountered. Imagine, bewitched by a strange white cat! We were both blissed out! She held me with her paws and eyes for several minutes, then curled up on my lap purring, letting me happily stroke her.

Later, when I got up to leave, the cat deliberately turned her back to me. As I walked away, I looked back once and at that same moment she twisted her head and caught my eye. In the silence between us, her words entered my mind with the utmost clarity: *I enjoyed that*. Then she turned away, dismissing me in a very catlike manner.

A connection on this level provides far more than mere physical enjoyment, yet all it requires of us is that we be open to life's subtle inner movement.

❀　　❀　　❀

Back in Oz a few years ago, Treenie and I and a couple of friends took a walk in a rain forest not far from where we lived. Afterward, our friends Graham and Helen invited us to their home for refreshments. As we drove down the narrow, winding road following their car deeper into the subtropical valley, the green lushness seemed to gradually close in on us. Wild lemons and guavas hung over the road, interspersed with dense thickets of flowering lantana, all competing with the heavy growth of cotton vine that seemed determined to clamber over everything.

We were driving slowly, when a few large, black-veined, golden-winged monarch butterflies flitted into the road. I slowed even more, but one of them hit our windshield and stuck for a moment. I put on the wipers for one sweep, and thought no more about it.

Reaching our destination, I parked some yards from Graham and Helen's house. Twenty minutes later, Treenie and I were sitting on their sun deck, sipping cold lemonade and deeply involved in conversation. I was totally immersed in what Graham was saying, when suddenly, like a touch of ice in the very center of my mind, came a single word: *Help!*

Without thinking, I leaped to my feet and raced to the car. There the butterfly fluttered one wing, trapped by an antenna under my windshield wiper. With great care, I lifted the wiper blade, and the butterfly soared free.

As I stood watching, mesmerized, it fluttered around my head and face for about a minute before lifting on the breeze and flying away. It was one of the most powerful moments of my life.

I suspect that practically everyone has been involved with a living creature in a way that has left him or her richer for the experience. This is particularly so for children.

Our youngest son, Russell, was nearly eleven when he,

Treenie, our daughter, Tracy, and I visited the Findhorn Foundation commune in Scotland. We were staying in Cluny House at the time, and I had been invited to give an evening talk on the Spirit of Nature at Drumduan House about a mile away. We were driven that afternoon along a winding road through a thick pine forest, past cottages nestled snugly into protective clusters of trees, and to our destination.

Russ and Tracy had planned to stay during the evening until my talk ended, and then return with us, but Russ, quickly bored, decided as it grew dusk to return to Cluny House. A resident told us that there was a fire track through the forest to Cluny—a shortcut—and he showed Russ where it was. I was hesitant to let him go alone as the evening grew darker, but Russ pleaded and I acquiesced.

It was the next day before he could share his experience with us. He had started walking along the fairly wide fire track, but as the evening gloom got deeper and scarier in the forest, Russ decided to run. As he nervously increased his speed, wishing fervently that he was not alone, a deer stepped out of the trees on the other side of the track and ran alongside him, keeping pace with him. To his great pleasure and astonishment, the deer stayed with him for the entire journey, quietly vanishing back into the forest as Russ reached Cluny House gardens.

The beautiful part is that Russ felt protected and cared for and the incident has left him open to the wonder and awe of life. What a gift!

14

A Story With a Sting

Let me tell you the story about the paper wasps that decided to make our front window frame their new homesite. Paper wasps are black, slim, bee-length insects, not unfriendly, and their first few flat, mushroomlike nests made of what seemed like chewed paper were hardly noticeable high on the window frame.

Fly screens over the windows kept us unbothered by wasps flying indoors, so a season of their reproduction passed almost unnoticed. But well into the second season, the window frame was becoming thick with their nests, some overlapping the glass. The frame filled, and the wasps blithely spread out over the wall, their numbers steadily increasing. Although close to our front door, the wasps returned our tolerance for them in good measure, for despite regular air traffic, none of our family got stung.

I rather enjoyed watching them; they were endlessly active, forever building new nests and caring for the young. Like bees, when the temperature rose too high for their nests, they clung to the hexagonal cells and fanned the heat away with blurred wings. And then I learned something surprising—they hunted. Unlike bees, they did not seek nectar; they hunted like true predators for other insects. And I noticed something else. It was normal each summer for us to be bothered by the usual swarms of small flies, for our home was surrounded by green pastures and fat cattle—but that season the flies were hardly noticeable.

With ruthless efficiency, the wasps caught and stung the flies, paralyzing and sealing them in their cells as living food for the growing grubs. Only then did I realize that, knowingly or not, we had developed a symbiotic relationship with the paper wasps. All in all, a most acceptable give-and-take.

For the next season, the relationship continued harmoniously, but the following year, Lance Rose, our landlord, decided it was time to paint the exterior of the house. I offered my assistance. Lance knew that I actively supported the wasps, so in unspoken agreement we painted and finished practically all the house until there was only one small wall with two windows left—and a lot of paper wasps!

Lance cleared his throat. "So, what are we going to do about the wasps? Shall I sweep them off, or what?"

I grinned. Lance and I got on very well. He was an ex-timber man and farmer, and was unusually open to Nature—certainly more than most of his peers. He had tolerated my idiosyncrasy toward the insects with well-veiled amusement. Aware of this, I described my strategy:

"We've obviously got to clean the wall and window frame before we paint it," I replied, "but I don't want to destroy the wasps. My plan is to paint a flat piece of board the same color as the walls. When it's dry, I'll transfer as many nests as possible onto it and hang it under the myrtle trees until we've finished the rest of the painting. Then I'll fix the board above the window so it matches the wall, and the wasps can continue to live on it. What I'll need from the wasps, of course, is an agreement that they will stay on the board and not build onto the window frame or wall again." I looked Lance in the eye, expecting some mild ridicule.

"Hmmm," he muttered, "and how do you intend to fix the nests onto the board?"

I smiled at him, "I haven't figured that out yet."

His eyes gleamed with a spark of solemn mischief as he considered the problem. "Why don't you hammer a whole lot of nails partway into the board. All you have to do then is jam a nest onto each nail and it'll stay in place."

I had no better solution, so I painted the board and, when it was dry, hammered in the nails. Later that evening, I put my proposal to the wasps. While I cannot say that they buzzed with enthusiasm, they really had no choice. Somehow I also got the clear message that they should not be moved until four o'clock the following afternoon when it was cooler and shady on the nests.

Although my deal with the wasps included a "no-sting" clause, my rather waspish lack of faith compelled me to take some minor precautions. I borrowed a bee net to protect my face, and some thin gloves for my hands, and at the appointed time climbed a short ladder to the nests.

Each small, platelike nest was secured to the window frame by an inch-long, papery column, so one by one I snapped them off and pushed them onto a nail. For a few moments, the wasps went crazy, rising in a buzzing, angry cloud around me. After giving me one needle-hot jab on the jaw, as though to prove the inefficiency of my defense, they suddenly became quiet and docile. It was remarkable.

I worked rapidly, clearing all the nests from the window

frame and a good many from the wall, fixing them with haste onto the nails. When the board was full, I carried it down the ladder and hung it under the tree only a couple of yards away. Then I hosed down the wall, destroying all remaining nests, and washed and prepared it for painting the next day.

The following morning, Lance and I finished the job. I returned the wasp nests on their board to their new site in the shade just above the window frame, with what I hoped was a clear understanding. Within days, the nests were resecured with new columns, and paper wasp life continued normally.

The paper wasps lived exclusively on the board, keeping the agreement until the following year when some late season wasps set up a few nests directly below the guttering. I left them alone—besides, I had told them not to nest on the wall or window frame; they must have considered the fascia board fair game.

It was only after several seasons of paper wasps that I really connected with their ethereal energy. When I had made our agreement and moved them to their new nesting site, I had felt little real contact with them—except, that is, for the sting on my jaw!

Now, I clearly felt the spirit of Nature in the consciousness of the paper wasps as I received an easy, silent flow of communication:

You can learn much by understanding wasps, they told me. *Take the sting on your jaw as an example. When a wasp attacks a human, it does so for a single purpose—to defend itself by protecting the swarm. Humans, however, defend themselves by attacking other people. In a similar manner, the paper wasp accumulates for itself by accumulating for the swarm. Humans accumulate for themselves by taking from other people.*

Paper wasps prosper by living in harmony with Nature, while humanity becomes impoverished by working against Nature. The paper wasp knows itself not as an individual entity, but as part of the consciousness of the swarm. Humanity knows itself only as an individual entity, unaware of the One human consciousness.

Life reveals that within the spirit of Nature there is great wisdom. Simple—yet profound.

15

The Ladies Have It

I realize it is remotely possible that you might have difficulty believing that the spirit of Nature can communicate with us. Let me assure you that it can, and does. When Treenie and I lived in Tasmania, I became well known as an organic gardener. An organic gardener grows plants in harmony with Nature by fertilizing the soil with natural products. This is in stark contrast to the harmful practice of directly stimulating plants with factory-produced chemicals.

For almost a year, in my capacity as an organic gardener, I was a regular guest on radio 7LA, a talk show hosted by Jane Stark on the subject of organic gardening. We had a lot of fun, sparking a tremendous local response. Often, I touched on the controversial issue of talking to plants. This is something in which I believe; after all, a splendid tree is just as likely to speak in humanese as a cat or dog.

I never ceased to be surprised at the number of people who, feeling safe in their anonymity, phoned to tell us of their personal experiences in this area. Their techniques were fascinatingly different and sometimes hilarious. While I had no proof that any of the accounts were true, I believed them. The speakers had a certain ring of credibility, and my own experiences provided ample validation.

Is it strange that with one exception, all of the incidents

described involved women and were volunteered by women? As an international seminar leader and speaker, I have observed that women definitely outnumber men when it comes to having an open mind. Generally speaking, they are more receptive, more aware, and far more intuitive, and they trust their intuition. Sorry, guys!

One of our callers described a beautiful creeping miller's dust that grew alongside the path to her front door. Unfortunately, in its enthusiasm the plant grew over the path as well, invading it from both sides, thus gradually reducing the safe walking area. Because the lady and her husband were rather elderly, this made the path dangerous for them. She cut it away regularly, a tough job. One afternoon, her back aching, she decided enough was enough. "Okay, you nuisance plant," she said, "that's it. I've had enough. If you grow over my path anymore, much as I love you, I'll dig out every last piece of you and take you to the rubbish dump."

That was three years ago, she told us, and the plant never again grew over the path. It did become a bit of a pest growing onto the lawn, but, as she said, "The lawn mower easily deals with that."

Another caller told us about a vigorous ivy with splendid mottled leaves that grew in a large container in her bathroom. Her great indulgence each day was to soak in the bath for half an hour as soon as the kids had gone to school. "I'm ready to face the day then," she told us. "While I'm lying in the bath, I talk to the ivy and tell it how beautiful it looks, and how much I love it.

"One day, I decided to see if I could persuade the ivy

to creep its way right around the bathroom, following the line where the walls meet the ceiling. So each morning I told the ivy what I wanted, and to my surprise it did it. It grew away from the window light, and over the next eighteen months it crept right around the bathroom. The ivy looks fantastic, and now it's on its second circuit!"

She must have been a very persuasive lady to get an ivy to grow away from natural light.

The lone man who phoned in had a question for me. "How do I get a tree to flower that hasn't ever flowered?" he asked.

"How old is it?" I asked him.

"Oh, I dunno. About twelve years perhaps."

"What variety of tree is it?"

"I haven't the faintest idea."

We went through a question-and-answer routine that yielded absolutely nothing of any value. Then I had an idea. "Do you like the tree?"

"No! Can't stand the bloody thing."

"And why is that?"

"Well, for one thing, me mother-in-law gave it to us, and for another, it never has any flowers."

Back to where we started! "Does your wife like the tree, or your kids?"

"No. Nobody likes it. I told you, it never bloody well flowers."

"How would you like it if nobody liked you?" I asked him. "Do you reckon you would be able to thrive and flower?"

Silence.

"Are you still there?" I asked.

"Yes, I'm here. That's a silly bloody question. I ain't a tree. I've got feelings."

"So have plants, which has been proved in laboratory experiments. Anyway, you rang asking for my advice. I suggest you have a good look at that tree and see if you can find any redeeming factors that will allow you to feel good about it. Try telling the tree how good it looks and that you're glad it's in your garden."

"But I ain't glad. I'd have chopped it down years ago, but the wife's mother would bloody murder me."

"You have nothing to lose by trying what I suggest. You may even get a surprise."

"Yeah! Surprise would be the bloody word." With this final surly comment, he hung up.

Five months later, he phoned again. I recognized his voice immediately. "G'day. Remember me? I'm the bloke who phoned about that tree that wouldn't flower."

"Yes, I remember."

"Well, mate, I'm telling you that tree is now in full flower. It's bloody beautiful. I want to say thanks."

It was my turn to be surprised. "I thought you hated the tree."

"Yes, I did. When you told me to try to like it, I thought you were bloody simple. But the wife heard what you suggested and reckoned we ought to try it. We had a good look at the tree, and I told her it was like a racehorse — it had good form. Ha, ha! She reckoned the leaves were nice, and we both liked the shade it gave. So I told the tree that it wasn't so bad after all. It's the truth — the tree seemed to perk up almost straightaway. And now she's a bloody beaut!"

Probably my favorite of all the stories I heard was from a caller who identified herself as "a little elderly lady who loves trees." Among the many trees in her garden was a magnificent apple tree. For years it had not borne a single apple.

"Each year I waited anxiously while it flowered, smothered in a profusion of pink and white blossoms, but never an apple," she told us. "Last year," she said, "I got my late husband's ax out of the garden shed, and carried it across the lawn to the apple tree while it was in full flower. I showed the ax to the tree and I said, 'I may be little and old, but if you don't have any apples on this year, I'll chop you down if it takes me a month!'"

At our end of the phone, we burst out laughing.

"Don't laugh," she said primly. "I had so many apples on the tree last season I hardly knew what to do with them. What's more, I told the tree that the same rules applied this season. And the tree is already loaded again!" Her words ended on a tone of triumph.

✿　✿　✿

During the time I lived at the Homeland commune, Yvonne, another member, asked if I would design a garden layout and help her plant a few shrubs around her new house. A few weeks later, we planted, basing our design on the universal yin/yang symbol for negative/positive, feminine/masculine: ☯.

It proved to be a real education for me.

From the beginning, both Yvonne and I were clear about which was the yin section of the garden and which was the yang. The yin was farthest from her bedroom window,

91

the yang closest. Around the yin section we planted tall, white-flowering, vigorous shrubs, while around the yang perimeter we planted equally vigorous red-flowering shrubs. For the inside of the circle, we planted species of low-growing natives using the *same* varieties in both the yin and yang sections.

My whole design was based on accomplishing the universal balance of yin/yang. I was in for a shock.

From the very first day, the yang section thrived, all the shrubs growing in a very desirable manner. The yin half was a calamity. Without exception, the shrubs drooped and languished, struggling to survive, while an identical plant of the same species grew prolifically only a few feet away in the yang sector.

There was no logical reason for this, yet the answer was quite simple. This was Yvonne's garden and received her focus and energy while she tended and cared for it, and, in those days, Yvonne was powerfully yang in her self-expression. Over the years, she became more balanced and the shrubbery faithfully reflected that. The yin section grew with increased vigor and far greater health.

Observing and understanding this phenomena took no great brain work. All it required was being open to the connectedness of life. We not only influence each other, but *all* life.

Following this line of speculation, can you even begin to imagine the implications for agriculture and the consciousness of nations on a global scale?

16
An Act of Courage

I lay on the ground, my head cradled comfortably on my arms, gazing up into the clear sky. Ten thousand feet above me, I watched a small plane follow its invisible flight path.

"They're out!" a distant voice shouted.

Squinting into the glare, I watched a number of tiny specks readily grow larger as they hurtled through the air on a rapid, downward trajectory. One of them was my son Adrian.

I reflected on my lack of worry. Unquestionably, I would rather he did not pursue such a precarious hobby as sky diving, but I did not worry about him. I liked the feeling of freedom it gave me. Watching him prepare for the jump, noting his careful folding of the high-tech parachute, seeing the smaller backup chute, and knowing that beneath all the superficial joking and clowning as he and his mates made ready was a whole lot of training and preparation had helped me accept it.

Lying back, marveling at how the sudden burst of his opening parachute seemed to snatch him back momentarily, I thought about his courage. Now, after well over five hundred jumps, I suspect it has become routine, but the first time he must surely have questioned his sanity and his motives; and he must surely have endured the terrifying thought, *what if the parachute.* . . . But he jumped anyway. That takes courage.

As I watched him land easily on his feet, the parachute billowing around him, I was aware that courage comes in many different forms. I thought of Molly. Let me tell you about her.

Treenie and I met her in Melbourne, Oz, where I was to give some talks and seminars. It was a cold, blustery winter day when we joined Peter and Denise, both of whom were organizers of my seminars, for tea and cakes in a little tea shop in Albert Park. Afterward, as is customary with most of the people I mix with, we stood for a moment on the pavement outside the shop sharing hugs, when an elderly woman passing by stopped, an involuntary exclamation bursting from her lips: "Oh, how I would love a hug!" Even as she spoke, she looked astonished at hearing her own words.

Treenie immediately broke away from us, and walking over to the stranger, embraced her warmly. As I watched, a look of extreme embarrassment crossed the woman's face, to be instantly replaced by an expression of intense joy.

"My God, I don't know what came over me! Oh, dear! I never talk to anyone in the streets. What have I done?" She was nervous, flustered, and shaken, but it was obvious she craved affection, really needed love.

When Treenie released her, I gave her a big hug. She was all rigid tension that melted as she relaxed. "Oh, God, I haven't had a hug like that in over ten years. I so needed to really be hugged," she whispered, tears in her eyes.

Both Peter and Denise hugged her in turn, while the

poor woman tried to excuse herself for being so rude as to ask for a hug. "I don't know what came over me," she said over and over, her face expressing her agitation.

In a nervous rush of words, she told us her name was Molly, and that she suffered from agoraphobia. It took her ten minutes to pluck up the courage to go outside the door of her flat. Just walking down the street was an ordeal. She was on her way to the hairdresser's, and it would take her up to twenty minutes simply to gain the courage to open the door and walk in. For her to speak to us about a hug was an incredible departure from her normal, hurried dash through the streets.

With sudden inspiration, Treenie said, "What you need is to come and hear Michael speak at the Town Hall tomorrow night."

"Oh, no! Oh, I couldn't possibly," Molly gasped.

"Let me make it easier," Peter cut in. "If you want to come, I will send a taxi to pick you up and we will make sure you are delivered home afterwards, right to your door at no expense to you. You will be our special guest." With that, he and Denise left us to keep another appointment.

"Oh, dear, how very kind you all are. But I couldn't possibly manage it," Molly said. "Oh, dear—" and she stopped, trembling with anxiety.

Lovingly, Treenie reassured her.

"Why are you so kind?" Molly asked. "I'm not used to so much love from perfect strangers. Most people don't care, or don't have time."

"We do care," Treenie said firmly. "We do have time."

"Do you know, it's the strangest thing," Molly said then,

gaining confidence, "a couple of weeks ago, I was having tea with my daughter-in-law, and a friend of hers called in. She is supposed to be an expert at reading tea leaves. She looked into my cup and told me that very soon I would meet a lady and a gentleman who would change my life."

She stared at us, wide-eyed. "Do you know, I believe that you are the lady and gentleman."

She went on to tell us that her husband had died eleven years earlier. Molly had lived totally for him. She had been so submerged in him, in his identity, that when he died there was nothing left of her or for her. She went to pieces. She had to be sedated and hospitalized, her sanity was threatened. That was when the agoraphobia began. Since then, she had stabilized to a certain degree, but the overwhelming loneliness and fearfulness had never left her. Living was a day-to-day endurance test.

"Listening to Michael is just what you need," Treenie coaxed. "Your tea leaves spoke of us changing your life, but you have to help that happen."

"I don't think I could possibly get in a taxi. It would take me all day just to get the courage," she said. For a moment, she looked thoughtful. "What did you say Michael would be talking about?"

I looked into her eyes. "Love."

"Oh, dear! If there is one thing I need to hear about and learn about right now, it's love. I know I don't even like myself, never mind above love. Oh, dear." Her voice was wistful and tears had come back to her eyes.

"We have to go now," Treenie told her. "Tomorrow night a taxi will come for you, and I will be waiting outside at the entrance to the Town Hall. I promise that I will hold your hand and look after you every moment of the evening."

"Oh, dear. I want to come," Molly said softly, the tears brimming in her eyes. "I want to come so badly—but I can't make any promises."

We hugged and kissed her, told her we loved her, and left her teary eyed on the pavement outside the tea shop.

The following evening, a trembling Molly tottered out of the taxi outside the Town Hall. Holding her hand, Treenie took her into the elevator and up to a large room buzzing with the conversation of about eighty people. I watched the two of them sit down together in the front row, and was concerned when the biggest man in the room sat on Molly's other side. I actually considered asking him to swap seats with someone smaller, but intuition told me he was okay. By the end of the evening, I had come to realize that Avo, the large man, was also probably the most gentle. He was as attentive to Molly's needs as Treenie.

For the entire length of my talk, Molly's eyes never left my face. Of all the people there, I spoke to her, heart to heart. I talked about loving ourselves, caring for ourselves, and knowing that we are each very worthwhile.

When the program ended, Treenie and I took Molly home. She was trembling so much from the effort of the evening that she would have fallen getting out of the car without assistance. We took her to her front door, watched while she unlocked and opened it, then we hugged and kissed her and bade her farewell. We never saw Molly again.

As we drove home, I reflected on Molly's courage. Every act we take for granted outside our home was an act of courage for her. Just entering a hairdresser's salon probably took as much courage for Molly as for Adrian to leap from ten thousand feet. I thought about her getting into the taxi, entering an elevator, being in a crowded room for an entire evening, and managing to endure the company of strangers for over three hours. For an agoraphobic, that's a whole lot of courage.

Treenie told me afterward that she was acutely aware of Molly's late husband being present during the program, and of feeling his great approval for what was happening. In a guided meditation, Molly told us that she heard the words: *It's time to let go, Molly love, it's time to let go.*

Whether or not we changed her life, I will never know, but she certainly had an effect on mine. For quite a while, I had been questioning my motives for continuing to speak in public. I am naturally a sensitive person. I am not the hail-fellow-well-met, life-and-soul-of-a-party type. In fact, it is doubtful I would even be at the party! I no longer had the need to hear my own voice as ego fodder. I no longer used speaking as a form of self-gratification. My question to myself was: Does my public speaking contribute toward the enrichment of the people who attend? And it was a serious question.

My experience with Molly suggested that I did, indeed, have something of value to contribute in the way of personal empowerment. So I now speak to Molly in each audience. Life met her need and mine in a simple, yet powerful manner.

17
Labels Without Meaning

One of the more difficult lessons I have encountered in life has to do with success and failure. I have had to learn that those terms are part of the brainwashing of youth, the imprints of school, the rhetoric of parental concern for the welfare of their offspring, the conditioning of a judgmental society.

When Treenie and I emigrated to Oz, we continued in the only way of life we knew—farming. In retrospect, I continued to farm not because it was the only thing I wanted to do, but because it was the only thing I believed I could succeed at.

Within a few months, we had bought a hill farm in Tasmania with the intention of becoming beef graziers. (The idea of being a beef baron tickled my fancy.) Life, however, had other plans. In our first year there, we experienced the worst outbreak of army-worm caterpillars the region had known in thirty years.

Caterpillars filled our water holes, polluted and poisoned the water, and stripped our pastures of every blade of grass and every leaf of clover. They lay thick on the ground as wave after wave crossed the railway lines. Local trains were forced to a halt, skidding and spinning on the crushed and greasy bodies. As a consequence, in that very first year we lost half our cattle to poisoned water. I classified this as *my* failure, even though common sense indicated that I could not be responsible for the vagaries of the weather.

After borrowing money from the Development Bank, we then commenced dairy farming. It took me less than eight weeks to learn that I detested milking, but eight long years before it came to an end.

You may well ask why we did not sell the farm if I disliked it so much. Following directly on the caterpillar plague, Tasmania had three consecutive years of the worst drought on record. Cold, dry winters slid into hot, dry summers, and every day was a struggle to survive. During all this—as though we needed another blow—a savage rural recession set in, made worse by a nationwide city boom. The price of milk, cream, and beef plummeted to an all-time low. Nobody, but nobody, was buying farms. The recession was to last on and off, mainly on, for six very difficult years.

How we held on through all the hardship, I don't know, but we did. The farm even grew when I purchased another 240 acres on borrowed money in an effort to survive. In those early days, the bank manager twice advised me to sell at the first opportunity, but to me that meant one thing—I had failed, and all my farming relatives and in-laws back in the U.K. would say, "Ah, they failed then. I told you that's what would happen if they emigrated. I knew no good would come of it."

I could not handle that. I needed their approval. In my role as a victim, I aligned myself with the years of conditioning that judged my efforts either as successful (hanging on meant I was successful) or, horror of horrors, a failure.

But during the struggle in those years of hardship, a change was taking place in me. I was becoming one of the pioneers of organic farming in Tasmania, an innovator — and so, in a natural organic way, my self-worth also flourished. Gradually, I came to realize that my fear of failure was exactly that — fear. I learned that failure is an expression of self-fear, while success is no more than the expression of self-confidence. Success and failure are simply labels, but labels that hide the real contents of the package.

As each year passed, I grew ever more aware of my previously unrealized abilities, and the value of my wonderful relationship with Treenie. Our four children also helped me develop as a human being, for the parent who does not grow with his or her children is sadly lacking.

By the time the recession ended, we had bred our cattle back into an excellent beef herd, finished milking, reduced our debts, increased the size of the farm, improved the health and vitality of the land and stock — and grown ourselves to a point where our confidence and self-expression were stretching the confines of agriculture.

At this point, selling the farm no longer meant failure. In fact, by the definitions of a fickle society, we had survived an agricultural holocaust. We were successful! But success and failure no longer held any meaning for us.

Life beckoned, and we had come to understand that life is an adventure to be lived, a mystery to be pursued, not judged or labeled.

18

A Ritual of Hope

In retrospect, I am grateful for the difficulties I experienced in my early years as an immigrant. Adverse experiences either make or break us, or, to be more accurate, we either find our depths and capabilities or slip uncomfortably into an apathetic state of self-pity.

During our years of regular bills and reduced, irregular income, Treenie and I faced many aspects of Self. At one stage, we had so many bills that I had only to open the desk and look at them to be instantly stricken with diarrhea. At times I was so worried that I lay awake at night sweating from sheer mental torment. I learned the *real* meaning of "worried sick."

I know for a fact that a few farmers, unable to deal with the pressure during those unrelenting years, committed suicide. Not that it helped. It just transferred the burden of responsibility to their long-suffering spouses. For me, Treenie was a tower of strength. If she was as worried as I was over the unpaid bills, she successfully hid it. While we paid our dribs and drabs to the merchants, we survived. Like most farmers, we got into the bad habit of self-denial. Any spending money we had went into either the farm or the children.

Nevertheless, on the epicurean side of life, we lived like proverbial kings. I had developed talents in self-sufficiency that kept a twenty-two-cubic-foot freezer filled with succulent goodies. The financial pressure, however, seemed unending and beyond my ability to cope with. Even when we had the occasional good financial year, it was swallowed up in a gulp just paying for the many poor ones. It seemed so unfair, for while I had no control over the price of our farm produce, my creditors gave every indication that my debts were my own fault.

It was during the very worst times, when I was whitefaced with anxiety, that we found a way to cope. Some of our land was two thousand feet above sea level in the foothills of Mount Arthur, high above the rest of the farm. Here, in this beautiful, open space, surrounded by dense forest, we could look out over the distant sea.

On a regular basis, when the pressure was too much, Treenie and I would drive up onto the highest point of our land and count our blessings. We deliberately switched our focus from what we did *not* have to everything we *did* have. It became a ritual, a badly needed immersion in all that was uplifting and positive.

"We have four wonderful children," we would affirm.

"We have good health and we have each other. We have an abundance of love in our lives. We have a lovely farm with healthy cows. We have fresh running water and plenty of pasture. We live in a truly beautiful place. We have many kind and generous friends. We have a life full of richness and blessings."

Blessings—that became the key. We had so many of those compared to the one thing missing—money.

Each time we went through this uplifting exercise, there

seemed to be more and more to be grateful for. The single "not enough money" became less and less threatening as we began to regain our power, which had been inadvertently surrendered to fear. We learned to count our blessings and, with conscious effort and deliberation, to focus on them in our daily lives.

As we practiced this, it became increasingly obvious that money was not as important as we had thought. What crippled us was not the lack of money, but our previous focus on what we lacked.

To this day, I am convinced that it was our changed perspective that changed our fortunes. Focus on the negative in your life, and it grows. Focus on the blessings, and they multiply. It is not luck, nor random chance, that determines the quality and content of our lives. It is, very simply, our focus.

19

A Misleading Cover

We all know the old saying "Never judge a book by its cover." The same saying applies to cassettes, and to most glossily marketed products today—and to people.

We know perfectly well that we should not judge people by their appearance, yet we do. It happens all the time—it has happened to me.

Treenie and I were in Phoenix to conduct a seminar. Tom and Linda, the program organizers, whom we had not yet met, picked us up at the airport. Tom is a big guy, an ex-lumberjack. Grabbing our two heaviest suitcases, he swung them lightly at his side as we followed him to the parking lot. "Don't know whether all this gear will fit in our little beetle," he said solemnly.

I didn't know how to respond. We followed silently. As we walked by a row of various cars, Tom suddenly swung the cases into the gaping maw of a huge Silverado. He looked at me, grinning boyishly at his little joke, while I sighed in relief.

I climbed up into the passenger seat, listening to Tom rattle off a list of engagements and details as he drove. He was still talking when I stopped listening and glanced at him surreptitiously, unwittingly judging the book by its cover. Then it happened. He wound down his window, leaned his head out, and spit!

It was my pet dislike—men who spit in public. (I have to say men, because I have yet to see a woman spit in public.) I groaned—silently. How could life organize for me to stay three weeks with a man who spit?

Later, sitting under the shade of a few large trees in Tom and Linda's backyard, I watched in amazement as Tom punctuated our conversation with a regular display of lengthy and remarkably accurate spitting. Linda was obviously embarrassed by the procedure, but it was something she was resigned to. Within a few hours, I learned that Tom not only spit, he also smoked and swore. Was it coincidence that I also dislike both these human habits?

When I went to bed that night, I asked the universe one question: "What in the hell am I doing here?"

Next morning, I lay in bed with a flow of clear insight surfacing in my mind. So far all I had seen in Tom were aspects I did not like. How about looking for ones I did? I had definitely judged the book by its cover; maybe it was time I had a good look at the contents.

I suppose I should not be surprised that the contents revealed a remarkable person. I found a man who matched me in his capacity to probe life for its hidden meanings. Like me, Tom was fascinated by the mystical aspects of life. Like me, he was dedicated to inner growth and committed to serving others. We were leaves from the same tree, and we both saw it. Tom was rare in being able to tell me, a comparative stranger, that he loved me. He put himself at my disposal for the entire three weeks, and nothing was too much trouble. When I asked him about his business as a reflexologist, he said, "That can wait. While you're here, I intend to learn from you and grow."

Learn he did, and grow he did, though painfully, for Tom resisted his growth process in the finest tradition. Like it or not, I seem to be rather a catalyst, and as his blocks came under my scrutiny, Tom triggered all the sequences his inner growth required.

He also gave Treenie and me one of the most powerful, and I must say painful, massages we have ever had, but we felt fantastic when it was over. And my feet, wow! He taught us how to really become acquainted with our feet, to experience the sense of well-being that stimulated, massaged, and relaxed feet provide.

The real Tom turned out to be a very sensitive person concealed under a cover of burly, growling manhood. I had to open the book to get past the cover, to find the contents of the real Tom. Just as a hermit crab hides in its shell, so Tom hid in his facade.

Seeing this allowed me to empty myself of those automatic inner programs that separate me from other people. In this, Tom helped me all he could—by carrying on with his smoking, spitting, and swearing—and I love the guy!

20
Quality Time

I was twenty-six years old when my father went into the hospital for an exploratory operation involving his bile duct. Afterward, the surgeon told my brother, Christopher, and me that Dad had cancer of the pancreas—and the bottom dropped out of my world. The cancer was inoperable and basically incurable—a death sentence. The doctor's estimate of nine months was to prove remarkably accurate.

The surgeon recommended, very strongly, that we not tell Dad or my mother about his condition. Knowing no better, we both agreed. I don't doubt the surgeon meant well, but today I consider such an approach little short of criminal; to presume that a person is unable to face the fact of death strikes me as the height of medical arrogance.

Naturally, I told Treenie about Dad's condition, and it was then that I went through my grieving process for him, while he was still alive. When he died, I was calm and detached. The initial shock had long since eroded. Daily, I had watched the effects of his cancer slowly ravage his fine mind and body, daily witnessed the shocking deterioration as he withered away.

The end came unexpectedly. I guess for most people death is always somehow unexpected, even when it is predicted. We were in his bedroom talking. He asked me for a drop of brandy, so I put my arm around his shoulders to support him while he sipped. He gave me the empty glass, sighed . . . and died. For a few bewildered moments, I did not realize he was dead, but as I gently laid him back on the pillow, it became obvious. Downstairs, several relatives were visiting, and I could hear the buzz of their conversation, but I sat quietly with Dad for another five minutes, watching his last involuntary breath fade away. Finally I said good-bye to him and went down to tell the family.

As was to be expected, grief, hysteria, and pandemonium broke out. I retreated. I felt no shock, no real sadness. For those last precious minutes, I had watched the imprint of prolonged suffering leave Dad's face, to be replaced by an expression of indefinable peace. I watched years fall away, as the deeply etched lines of his serious face eased and softened for the first time in so long. This was years before I made my own investigation into dying and death, but it was the trigger for my inquiry. In some ways, Dad's death seemed more like a coming alive, only he was no longer available to us.

Strange as it may seem, the last months of his life were some of the best *quality* time he and I ever spent together. Dad's father had died when Dad was only two years old, so he had no role model for how to be a father. I loved and respected him, but most of the time we were not good friends. We were father and son, with endless arguments between us. Toward the end, as he became more seriously ill, Dad had no energy left for bickering, and together we found acceptance of one another, and peace.

I am sure that, deep inside, Dad knew he was dying.

About six weeks before he died, an incident occurred between us that was to have a profound effect on my life. He wanted to share a few feelings, which he was not practiced at sharing.

I can never remember Dad saying he loved me. Like so many men, he found it impossible to speak words of love to someone of the same sex, even a boy. I have a very clear memory of him picking up Josephine, the girl next door, when she was about six years old and I was about eight, and telling her he loved her. I remember the pain I felt. I so badly wanted him to say those words to me.

On this particular afternoon, Dad began hesitatingly to tell me that he had misjudged me. He was always one for proverbs and popular sayings, and I can still hear him saying, "Ever since you were a boy, I've had to keep reminding myself that wild colts make the best horses."

He went on to apologize for comparing me academically with my brilliant brother. "Since you got married, I've seen a side of you I didn't know existed," he said, confessing how he had failed to appreciate the qualities in me he was now trying to acknowledge.

He tried groping uncertainly into his deeper feelings of affection for me. How desperately he tried to tell me he loved me, but the words defeated him. And sadly, I was as unpracticed as he, so the words were never spoken between us; but we both knew and felt the love that bonded us.

That afternoon of reaching out to each other was a triumph of quality time. The fact that we could not share the words of love produced a lasting impression. I was a father myself, of Duncan and Adrian. Silently, I vowed then and there that for as long as I lived I would tell *all* my family how much I loved and appreciated them. And I do. I never leave it to be taken for granted. My three boys are grown men now, but when I meet them or we talk on the phone I tell them—as easily as I tell my daughter, Tracy—that I love them. Just as easily, they can speak their love to me. How I value that.

To verbally declare our love to those we love is very simple, but so many people—particularly men—never do it. Nothing is more empowering to the declarer or to the recipient than the words "I love you." Nothing is more powerful. And nothing could be simpler.

There is always a reward in sharing our love, and sometimes there is an extra bonus.

Only a month before Treenie and I left Oz for our United States tour, Russell married a lovely girl named Michelle. During the planning stages, Russ asked me to be his best man. Silly as it seems, I was vaguely embarrassed.

"Can't you choose between Duncan and Adrian?" I asked.

"Yes," Russ replied. "I could if I wanted to."

"You know it's normal to use one of your brothers, or your best friend," I said.

"Yes, Dad, I know," Russ replied patiently. "That's why I'm asking you."

I hugged him, tears in my eyes, memories of my father and myself swimming through my mind.

I was best man, and I loved it. When, during the speeches, it was my turn to say something, I told the story of my father and me. I talked of sharing love, and how I, Russell's father, had reaped the honor of being his best man. While I was speaking, you could have heard Dad's proverbial pin drop, so total was the attention.

Later, no less than six men shyly told me how deeply my words had affected them.

This was in a farming community, where men are often out of touch with their deeper feelings. One confided that he had four grown sons and he had never once told them he loved them. Then, ten years ago, a surprise last son was born. By now the older man had mellowed and matured enough to be able to tell this son how he felt. Recently, his grown sons had returned home for some family occasion and, for the first time, he had said, "I love you," to them. His eyes were misty, describing how his sons had cried, saying they had waited all their lives to hear him speak those words.

Becoming a mother or father is a biological happening that a whole lot of people manage to accomplish. Being a *responsible* parent is something quite different, requiring we grow with our child, which requires that we be open to growth. To be a parent *and* best friend is something else. Probably more than anything, what's needed here is to find humility. Perhaps even to be able to say, "I'm wrong," when we are, in fact, right! Why? Because being a friend is more important than being right. Rights and wrongs will sort themselves out, but real friendship does not wait. It has to be an all-the-time thing. Best friends are chosen, not inherited.

Another equally important ingredient in being both parent and friend is the ability and the willingness to communicate openly. Open communication creates quality time. Sadly, something as simple as quality time has become all too rare.

21

Litany of Spite

I am often asked about destiny. Do I believe life is preordained, or do we choose our life's path? This is a question I do not take lightly. When I am asked it, my memory invariably serves up an incident from my youth. As I reflect on that incident, shaping my answer, I recognize that most of humanity lives in such a permanent state of unawareness that choice is not possible. We cannot choose a path in life if we are unaware of other paths, of other choices. We cannot pick the single red apple from a basket of green ones if we are color-blind.

But suppose the single red apple chooses us, what then? Impossible, you say. But are you sure? Because if you are wrong, your freedom to choose in life is seriously curtailed.

Let me tell you about that incident from my youth, because probably more than any other moment in my life, it affected my destiny. It took place on my father's farm, when I was nineteen years old. It had rained for several days, but was clear now, with a warm, drying wind. I was using a long-tined pitchfork to turn damp rows of straw in a harvested field, so the straw would dry prior to baling. My companion, Stan, was a man probably forty years my senior, one of the laboring class in a very class-conscious England, a man embittered by his life's experience of inequality. Few people knew as deeply as I how bitterly he resented this discrimination.

From the time I commenced work on my father's farm at age fifteen, Stan had used me as his outlet for the deep-seated anger and humiliation he had accumulated over a lifetime of servitude. It took the form of verbal violence, not so much directed at me personally, but at my paternal grandmother and her family. She was an obvious target, for she was strong willed and dominant, and liked to put folks in their place—or, should I say, the place she thought they belonged!

Stan's diatribes were a subtle violence, psychologically disturbing for both of us. My family were very closed people, never volunteering their history to me, never discussing family indiscretions with me. My ignorance of the truth made me vulnerable to Stan's malice, lies, and half-truths.

In retrospect, I realize that his hostility caused him to feel guilty because he was very fond of my father. Paradoxically, he also had a real affection for me, but his class hatred was too great for him to surmount.

It is difficult to convey the effect of being regularly subjected to a vindictive and demoralizing onslaught, especially when my tormentor was so much older that a fight was not an honorable alternative. During this time, I never confided in my parents, or anyone else. I endured it for four years, holding my rage deep inside me, fearing the consequences of its emergence.

On this particular day, as we worked in the welcome sun, the faint crackling of drying straw mingling with the song of skylarks, an unnatural bleakness swept through me when

Stan began his corrosive litany of spite. I do not know why, but on this occasion I felt a sudden upsurge of uncontrollable violence and outrage. He had stopped his work and was staring at my back. I could feel his eyes boring into me, a familiar feeling. He made another cutting remark, this time more personal, and I also stopped the regular rhythmic motion used to turn the rows of damp straw.

I felt something inside me shift, and my rage came flooding to the surface. I turned, and our eyes locked; he saw that he had gone too far, way too far. Fear and apprehension washed his face, draining it of color.

My feelings were entirely new. There was no thought, no red-hot anger, nothing but a seething cauldron of emptiness. Even the rage that precipitated this experience had vanished. I felt only the need to end it, to end him. With a couple of swift paces, I closed the distance between us and, lost in the emptiness, drew back my suddenly deadly pitchfork as a weapon.

In the fractional moment before stabbing forward with the two eighteen-inch tines, I saw the horror in his eyes, the dread. In that frozen moment, my body poised to unleash all my long-contained violence, I was flooded by what I can only describe as absolute love. Every cell in my body became light, tingling and vibrating. The emptiness of my heart and mind was instantly overflowing with the experience and knowledge of love. And love was not something I felt—I *was* love.

Even now I look back at the experience in wonder and with a sense of awe.

It seemed we were both immobile for ages, but it was

only seconds before I calmly lowered the pitchfork. Sweat beaded Stan's face; his eyes were still shocked. I think he may have doubted my sanity when I spoke. Listening with disbelief to my own words, I heard myself say, "It's okay now. It's over. You'll never be able to hurt me again with your spiteful words. You see, I love you and I forgive you."

The rest of that day was very quiet. He was withdrawn and subdued, while I was lost in embarrassment over what I had said, and overlighted by a sense of wonder and a fading experience of love that, sadly, I could not sustain.

The experience completely changed our relationship. Within a few months, Stan's tirades had ceased, though about two weeks after the incident he tried to reestablish his dominance. But his words of spite meant nothing to me now; they no longer had the power to hurt me.

Years later, when Stan died, it was easily and with dignity. I believe that I may have been partly responsible, for whatever happened to me also affected him. In some way, my love and forgiveness seemed to exorcise his own personal torment.

Which brings us back to destiny. At the moment I was about to kill, *something* intervened. Did that intervention change my destiny, or did it prevent me from changing it? You decide.

22

A Dream Made Manifest

I am convinced we manifest *all* the events in our life, major and minor. What we constantly think about becomes the main focus of our manifestation, though this may be unwitting and unknown. If we like the event made manifest, we consider ourselves lucky; if we don't, then we are unlucky. Either way, we are a victim of our own, unrecognized inner power.

This story is about the deliberate manifestation of a long held dream, knowing the rules and using them, and the unexpected confrontations this invoked.

In the early 1970s, Treenie and I were farming in Tasmania and going through a process of fairly intense change. Change seems to be the story of our life. We had heard and read about the inspirational community in Scotland known as Findhorn, and we, too, were inspired by their vision. We determined to end our farming career and join—or begin—a similar community in Australia.

Furthermore, we intended to manifest our communal dream. We wanted to live the concept of wholeness about which we had read and, in living it, make it real. The only snag was we had not a clue as to how to go about it.

We sold the farm in 1976, which took us out of debt, but we had not nearly enough money to buy any sort of property with which to commence our project.

We spent much of the year traveling around Oz. We entered our children in a correspondence school and traveled wherever the whim of the moment took us. Let me be honest with you—I was no bold and carefree traveler. Daily, I felt a growing sense of fear and inadequacy. Here we were, attempting to manifest a whole new commune-based life-style, and I hardly knew what we were doing or where we were going. All I knew in life was farming, and that was the one thing I would not be doing. Glaringly, I was confronted by my limitations, and daily the idea of us manifesting a commune seemed more absurd.

For me, the problem compounded. I say for me, because Treenie had none of my hang-ups—which made me feel even more inadequate. When we called in at a small commune near Mildura in New South Wales, in spite of the warm welcome we received, it did not take me long to realize that numbers of people was another threat. My exterior act of strong and easy confidence was just that—an act.

We were only there for about a week, but during that time, despite my fears, we made a deep connection with Art and Em Davis, owners of the commune's citrus and grape farm, and their family. Their two sons, Bruce and Mark, were particularly attracted to our vision of a commune.

Life brought us back to the Davis family late in 1976, and we settled down for a while into a routine. Bruce and Mark moved more strongly into our lives. They were personally fiercely competitive with each other, and also very different from each other. Bruce, a few years Mark's senior, was a dreamer in those days, not very practical, but, possessing a gift of words and often startling insight, he was a great inspirer of people. Mark was much more practical, very enthusiastic, and keen to see all work and projects finished on schedule. Bruce started jobs; Mark finished them.

As life became a routine, it was not long before Treenie and I began to feel the beginnings of discontent. We had shared our vision with these people, and Bruce and Mark wanted to be part of it, but nothing was happening. Art and Em were planning to sell their block (local grape and citrus growers were generally known as "blockies") and go overseas on a long overdue holiday; meanwhile, I felt we were just marking time.

One morning, I told Bruce that Treenie and I were thinking of moving on. Our dream was not coming together. We discussed it for some time, and slowly the real issue came to light—we had no direction. When would it happen? How? With whom? Where? We had a sense of purpose, but no framework in which to place it. Everything was vague and nebulous.

Out of our discussion came clarity, and with the clarity our prayer of manifestion was born. It was a prayer we believed in. As a group we read it daily, tuning in to its essence. This is the prayer:

Prayer of Manifestation
We are gathered together, Father, in your presence to ask for a Light Center.
We wish to invoke your energies to work through us in the manifestation of this Light Center.
We ask for and affirm our belief that we will receive the

money to acquire, or that in the way of the Holy Spirit we will receive what is needed for, a Light Center.

If it is God's will, we ask for an area near the East Coast, in the south Queensland area, with sufficient acres of fertile soil, that is also a power center filled with a life force waiting to be released through the kingdoms of humanity, Nature, and God in a blend of oneness and attunement.

We ask for an abundance of fresh, pure water, a supply that will never fail us through any adversities. We acknowledge the vast, untapped spiritual quality of water, and express our desire to draw closer in understanding the water kingdom and its infinite wisdom, as a link and sharing of life through God.

We ask that there shall be an abundance of trees of many varieties on this sacred piece of land. We affirm our love of trees and our contact with the intelligence of trees. We wish for the greatest attunement possible through this kingdom.

We ask for a large home with outbuildings on this land, so we have shelter while we build our family homes. We ask that the home will serve as a community center, as our Light Center unfolds under your loving guidance.

We ask for hills and valleys within our special area. We ask for the beauty and support of the mountains to be close by.

We ask that the incredible vibration and vitality of the ocean shall be near enough that we benefit from its spiritual presence.

We ask, Father, for these things to be manifested through your Holy Will. We bow before your infinite plan. We come before you in love, using our rights as creators to create a center of harmony to demonstrate the limitless love and truth of a new era.

*We ask for this to be manifested by the 1st of April, 1977,
when we will leave here, putting ourselves in your guidance
toward this, your Light Center.*

We thank you, Father.

As you will notice, this was no wishy-washy prayer. We
were very specific, but if God or life decreed otherwise,
then so be it.

❀   ❀   ❀

Time slipped by in a haze of ever increasing heat, and
one day Treenie felt very strongly that Bruce and I should
go looking for our special piece of land.

It was a bold move, and frightening, for we had little
money and we were proposing to put our faith on the line
by finding, and even starting legal purchase of, land we
only assumed we would find. In mid-November, only three
weeks after writing the prayer of manifestation, Bruce and
I left on the six-hundred-plus-mile journey to the East
Coast. We traveled in the Bluebird, Bruce's beat-up Holden
panel van.

Our first destination was the New Awareness Center in
Sydney, a group formed by Terrance Plowright, who had
returned from Findhorn to put his ideas and expression
into a form that would attract other, like-minded people.
We introduced ourselves to Terrance and outlined our
plans. He was friendly and receptive, but a bit distant.
Bruce had a remedy for this. After about ten minutes, he
leaped up and threw an arm around the startled Terrance's
shoulder. "Come on, relax, man. Don't be so uptight. We're
all pals, y'know!"

Terrance, rather shattered by this approach, visibly relaxed. Much later, we went home with him to his flat, and slept.

Next morning we met Betty, Terrence's gracious landlady. She also became enthusiastic about our quest, and helped us acquire some petrol, nearly unobtainable in Sydney owing to a strike. Without her help, our timing, which was crucial, would have been seriously jeopardized.

Our plan was to drive north to Noosa Heads, in southern Queensland, then slowly back down the coastal region looking for our special place. We had no attachment to the contents of the prayer of manifestation. Even if it proved to be a peninsula of sand, that was okay, so long as we knew with surety that it *was* our special place.

We took turns driving up the coast, a long, tiring day.

Later that night, ever a light sleeper, I twisted and turned in the back of the Bluebird, listening to Bruce groan in his sleep. We were in a grassy, sheltered nook, near trickling waters. Because of the masses of mosquitoes, I had insisted on keeping the windows closed to the merest crack.

Now we were both suffering. Bruce with his dreams of slow death by asphyxiation, I of thirst from eating too many prawns before retiring. My mouth had that old-socks feeling. Finally Bruce gasped, "Roadsie, I gotta have air. I'm suffocating."

Honestly, some people make such a fuss! Nevertheless, we tumbled out of the vehicle and, while Bruce indulged in deep breathing, I found a small creek and drank a few gallons, and felt fine.

❀　　❀　　❀

Curled to perfection, white tips caressed by a light wind, the waves came running up the beach. Bruce and I leaped out of the Bluebird, plunging into the sea with cries of delight. Soon, wet and salt encrusted, we drove on up the coast.

Bruce claimed to know the area, and at the end of the day headed us toward a promised freshwater river. I had serious doubts as the road became a rapidly deteriorating track, losing itself in lush jungle, but, sure enough, we hit the jackpot. It was perfect for washing away the salt of sea and sweat of travel.

We drove all day after an early morning swim. By the time we reached our destination, the changing scenery had become a blur.

In Noosa Heads, we called at a real estate agency and made plans to meet a representative the next day. An hour later, we drove into nearby Noosaville, hiring a trailer for the night to catch up on our sleep. Bruce was snoring gently when I put my book down. As soon as my eyes closed, all hell broke loose. Listening to the hubbub, I deduced that a football team of boys had camped here earlier, and had just returned from town. Several hours later, a cane toad hunt got under way. Shouts of profanity floated on the air as toads were stuffed into beds and down necks. Just as I was about to go berserk, a loud, irate voice threatened to neuter all of them. Apart from a few subdued mutterings, the threat produced the desired effect.

We awoke early, Bruce fresh from ten hours of deep, uninterrupted sleep, I groggy from lack of it, and went to meet the real estate rep, who asked us what we were looking for. Bruce opened his mouth to reply, then looked at me. That's when I became the spokesman for our hunting trip.

"Well, it depends," I said. "We'll know what we're looking for when we find it. Until then, let's see what land you have."

Six farms later, Bruce and I headed south. It took that long because of my attachment to the Queensland area.

Gradually, we worked our way down the coast from one township to the next, visiting one beautiful farm after another. Nothing, however, rang the inner bells of recognition. Not once did we feel that this was our special place. Eventually, taking an inland route, we drove down the steep, winding route from the high, cool altitude of the Dorrigo plateau, into the warm and humid valley of Bellingen.

By the time we found the Cedar's campground and booked in, the shops were closed, but this did not stop us from reading the advertisements for properties in the real estate windows. Soon after we settled in the trailer, Bruce and I agreed we were getting warmer. We both felt a keen sense of anticipation.

Just before dusk, as I was enjoying some more prawns, I noticed the large seedpods on some nearby trees begin to flap around. Startled, I looked closer and recognized them as huge clusters of flying foxes, large, foxy-faced fruit bats. I gave them my full attention. Only then did I see that they were hanging by the thousands in the clump of trees on a small piece of ground that had once been an island in the Bellinger river. Soon, Bruce and his camera were recording the scene as the bats screamed and swore at each other, stirring from the lethargy of sleep. When dusk fell, the night sky darkened with huge swarms of them spiraling into the surrounding gloom, searching for local flowers and fruit.

I shared the last of my prawns with a thin red setter who befriended me for just as long as the prawns lasted. Then she, too, disappeared into the evening.

The next morning, bright with promise, we joined Andy, another real estate agent, to continue our search for our special place. Bruce and I had a new feeling of excitement, which may explain why we were more forthright with Andy, sharing our plans in greater detail. He had actually heard of Findhorn. That was a surprise. Even though he knew nothing of its function, it made a good start. Andy seemed to understand what we needed, so when I told him, "Anything from one acre to three hundred, and when we see it, we'll know," he took it in his stride.

By the end of the day, we must have looked at a dozen properties. Some of them were beautiful farms, others just acreage with river frontage. Several could have met our needs, yet the magic of knowing had not happened. We were both a bit deflated when Andy said, "Well, boys, there's one more property to look at up the Darkwood road. She's a bit big, but I reckon it's perfect for what you need."

I was sitting in the front with Andy, while Bruce sat strangely subdued in the back. Since entering the Darkwood road, we had crossed the river once over a low, wood bridge, and we were about to cross again, as the river twisted its serpentine way through the valley. Noticing a deep swimming hole, Bruce and I chorused, "Whoa, Andy."

Andy watched grinning when we plunged in. God, I love rivers! "Are we anywhere near the farm?" Bruce asked him.

"One more bridge, boys, and we're there."

We climbed into his car, still wet, and continued along the narrow road. Clattering over the next bridge, Andy told us that the property lay on both sides of the road for nearly a mile. As he gave us the details, it sounded both impressive and expensive. The farm was for sale at $65,000, walk in, walk out. It had been a dairy farm until recently. The elderly owner now ran a few beef cows and calves.

The car swept along the road. Our eyes devoured the farm, the river flats, the dips and valleys, the trees on the hills, and the neat little farmhouse.

"Shall I stop?" asked Andy.

I felt nothing inside me, so I replied, "No, keep going." I did not glance at Bruce in the back of the car.

We looked at a couple more blocks of land, but the inner bells did not ring. We were soon back in Bellingen.

Bruce and I climbed into Bluebird, lost in our own thoughts. "What did you think, Bruce?" I asked.

He looked morose. "What did *you* think, Roadsie? How about the big farm we saw?"

I explained patiently that it was too expensive. Maybe, by some miracle, we might find half that money, but $65,000, no way.

He looked defeated. "What's wrong?" I asked him.

"Nothing, Roadsie, let's go home. We've blown it." He started the Bluebird and headed toward the Pacific Highway.

I sat stunned. What had gone wrong? What had we blown? By now, I also was angry and upset.

The Bluebird devoured the miles in our strained silence, and we were on the highway heading home, when I noticed a sign that read Hungry Head Beach pointing to our left.

"Go down there to the beach," I said. "We'll talk."

He swung round the corner in a spray of gravel and drove to the grassy headland, where we parked. We looked at each other in silence. "Okay, what's bugging you?" I asked him.

"Roadsie, we're not ready. We don't have the trust and faith to do what we have to do. We're too limited."

In some detail, he continued to tell me that he had been doing inner somersaults in the back of the car, silently screaming that this was it, as Andy drove us along the Darkwood road. Bruce had waited for me to recognize this as our special place and confirm his inner feelings. When I said, "No, keep going," he was devastated.

As he talked, I began to understand a bit more about myself. Talking about manifestation was one thing; facing it was something else. That was one part of the problem; the other part was my bogged down practicality. For all my life, I had been conditioned to deal with money in a logical, practical way. What we were proposing was neither logical nor practical. It was about trust and faith in the unknown. It was about practicing being limitless, instead of limited. When Andy said $65,000, my logic erected a barrier of impossibility. We did not have the money, we could not get the money; so what was the point of looking over the farm when it was not possible to buy it? I had to face a truth. Bruce had said, "Roadsie, we're not ready." The truth was, it was good old Roadsie who was not ready.

Nobody could have been less practical than Bruce in

131

those days. And at that moment, nothing was less needed than practicality. Although the money angle blocked me, I swiftly worked out a compromise. We would buy it and subdivide. We could keep what we needed and use the balance of money to begin a program of building. Good old brain, I knew you could do it!

We agreed to go back to the farm and reassess our feelings.

The next morning, I stood with Bruce on some high ground overlooking the farm. Inside I felt the veils of limitations being torn free to be swept away in the breeze. Inner bells were ringing and my heart was hammering as I finally realized—this was it! This *was* our special place. The pure confrontation of it all, the impossibility of it, was struggling to survive when Bruce, who had wandered ahead with his camera, called out, "Hey Roadsie! Wait till you see this lot."

I ran to catch up and, as I topped a small rise, the river lay below us like a huge sparkling necklace draped around the neck of an abundant Mother Nature. It was breathtaking!

Simultaneously, Bruce and I realized that everything we had written in the prayer of manifestation was in this property. There was more splendor and greater abundance than we had even imagined. My last doubts, along with all thoughts of subdivision, faded away. How it could happen, I did not know, but by God, we had found the place, and so, I trusted, happen it would.

Soon we were having morning tea with Jim and Ruby Cleaver, the owners. We assured them we would buy the property, and would visit Andy to finalize the deal. It was then that Jim dropped the clincher.

"That'll be fine, lads, but one thing I need to make clear. We want to visit our daughter in New Guinea fairly early next year, so you must take possession on April 1, 1977."

The prayer of manifestation was complete.

A little later, in Andy's office, we signed all the necessary documents. When all was in order he gave a satisfied smile. "You know boys, that property was priced at $100,000 until two days ago. Jim came in and said he wanted to sell quickly, so he dropped the price."

Bruce and I looked at each other, knowing that our time around Noosa Heads had not been wasted. My attachment to southern Queensland had held us there long enough for us to be here at the perfect time. I will never know if my limitations could have hurdled a $100,000 barrier!

We made arrangements to pay the ten percent deposit at the end of January 1977, and to take possession on balance of payment on the 1st of April, 1977.

On our way back to Sydney, Bruce and I alternated between elated chatter and long periods of silence, each of us lost in our own thoughts. More and more powerfully I could see the serendipitous unfolding of the past events. I still gasped at the thought of being part of a commitment to paying money we did not have; we couldn't even scrape up the deposit, never mind the rest! My logical mind screamed, you are mad; but another inner voice whispered, by faith, it can be so. Even the combination of Bruce and me was somehow perfect, for each balanced and complemented the other.

But my mind continually boggled at the sheer craziness of our situation. I was certain that if either Jim Cleaver or Andy had known what our reality was, they would have thrown a fit! And who could have blamed them? I had a feeling they would have had a whole lot less faith in our prayer of manifestation than we did.

The journey to Sydney seemed brief, so engrossed was I in thought and speculation.

❀　　❀　　❀

We had planned to leave for home early Monday morning after a night of Betty's hospitality, but Terrance remarked that the New Awareness Center was holding some workshops at the forthcoming Down to Earth festival at Canberra. Would we like to go?

I was torn. I badly wanted to get back to Treenie and the children, but I also wanted to experience a festival such as this. We decided to stay.

Two days later, we were at the Cotter Dam, a few miles from Canberra, the governmental capital of Oz. Imagine a deep valley cut into timbered hills. Place a clear, fresh river flowing in and around the valley, liberally dot the area with masses of brightly colored tents, and the scene is set. New Awareness had a site only a few yards from the cold river, set against a backdrop of rock. The next few days were, more than anything, a bonding between Bruce, myself, and the folks from the New Awareness Center.

Bruce and I helped in the workshops, talking about the Findhorn Australia commune we intended to start. I should state clearly here that Findhorn Australia was a term we used to identify our purpose and intent in those formative months. We were not related to Findhorn, Scotland, in any way, other than being inspired by their example.

During those few days at Cotter Dam, we were approached by several people who would eventually join us; notable among them was Anatole and his family, who had been planning to go to the Findhorn commune in Scotland. Thus, the seeds of our vision were sown in other people.

The long journey home from Canberra to Mildura passed quickly. Bruce and I alternated between driving, sleeping, and conversation. We had been away for twenty days, and it was wonderful to be home. I don't enjoy being separated from Treenie.

Sharing our adventures and experiences, it was a thrill to be embraced by the enthusiasm of the group. I, more than Bruce, needed that. Doubt and logic made a mockery of our plans; I needed reinforcement.

Christmas passed. Outside the air-conditioned house, it was so hot and the air so dry that we had to blink rapidly to keep our eyeballs moist. The family dogs collapsed in a panting heap, showing little sign of life until evening. Even the mosquitoes panted as they droned in for a bite, and the flies almost stopped flying. Hot, dry, and dusty—talk about contrast to beautiful Bellingen with its cool river!

We had a letter from Terrance shortly after Christmas suggesting that some of those at the New Awareness Center join forces with us. I think he considered this a revolutionary suggestion, but Bruce and I had both known it was inevitable.

Gradually, the days melted away, approaching the date our $6,500 deposit was due. Meanwhile, a Melbourne newspaper sent two reporters to write a story about us. We tried to share our dream with them, to get them to see the possibility of faith as a viable method of manifestation, but I suspect these reporters had no intention of listening. They wanted sensation, and sensation they wrote. The resulting article in the paper, entitled "Faith, Hope and $65,000," contained little more than a distorted interpretation of our words. However, if the article was an insult to our intelligence, at least it was not derogatory, so I guess we escaped lightly.

The jangling bell of the telephone rang constantly during January, as our Sydney friends checked in to find out if we had manifested the deposit yet. That tested me. I did not know how it would happen myself, never mind how to answer other people's queries.

I felt the burden of responsibility rather keenly. As a group, faith was high and fine. As individuals, uncertainty ruled. But Treenie was a tower of strength for me. It never seemed to enter her head that we might not get the money, or that our dream might not come true. To be honest, the thought seldom left mine; doubts haunted me.

But I hung in there. I could inspire others, if not myself, and they, in turn, inspired me. Crazy, but it worked. Our strength definitely lay in the group as a whole. In the group, there was faith. Faith and hope are so close, so alike, yet so very different. As an individual, I did not discover faith during this exercise in manifestation. For me, that came later. Faith is a movement of immense inner, yet universal, power, while hope is also sister to hopelessness. I discovered that the meeting place between hope and faith is trust. Trust is the handle by which to grip faith.

The week before the deposit was due, I had reached a

point where I believed in what we were doing, I believed it would happen, but I could not simply *trust* the process. I could not stop my practical mind from trying to work out *how* it would happen. I think most of us were like that. And there was no practical or logical answer. We had no choice but to trust—simply trust.

We had just finished dinner one evening, when the phone rang. It was Anatole, saying that he was sending us a check for $4,000 toward the deposit. Could we make use of it? Could we ever!

After that, it came together quickly. Pam, a young woman staying with us, had $2,000 saved for a trip to Europe. She now offered it to us, rightly trusting we could pay her back in time. Treenie and I dipped into our dwindling account for the last $500, and we had the deposit!

The manifestation of our deposit eased the grip of doubt and logic, and reaffirmed our faith. We were surprised to discover that we were our own miracle. Amazingly, manifesting that small amount of money had put us all through the wringer. In discussion, we found that we had each, in our own way, been confronted by our own personal shortcomings.

Not long before the grape harvest was due, Art found a buyer for his block who wanted to take possession on March 31, 1977. Talk about timing! Treenie and I headed for Sydney in mid-March, to park our small family trailer in Betty's driveway.

During the remaining few weeks before we took possession of the property, all those people who would join us came together. During this time, a lady of great wealth offered us the complete sum of money to purchase the land—with a condition attached to the offer. We discussed it, decided the condition was unacceptable, and politely declined. It seemed we were crazy. With no idea where the money would come from and, with the day of finalization rapidly approaching, we had just turned down the required money. Yet our faith was now stronger. The money had to be free of long-term conditions. We did not see the money as a gift to us; it was a gift to God. Idealistic, maybe, but we were very definitely sincere.

The money was a challenge we could not solve or face individually, so we organized a meeting. Everyone who had an interest in what we were doing was invited to participate, even if he or she was only vaguely curious.

The meeting got under way, with us sharing our ideas about how we would begin organizing the commune. We were reluctant to bring up the real issue—money. The spontaneous offer of donations prompted us to pass a pen and paper around the room of about thirty people. We proposed to accept all offers of donations as interest-free loans. Later, when we had settled on the land, people could make a choice as to whether their money was a loan or donation. At that meeting, and over the next two days, we received pledges of $40,000, an incredible statement of faith in our communal venture. We spent a few hectic days chasing the balance, finally taking a loan from the bank. On April 1, 1977, the property became ours. The name Homeland followed a few months later. A year later, our accounts showed that one-third of the money we had collected was an interest-free loan, one-third was an outright donation, and one-third was a loan from the bank. Within three years, we were debt free of the purchase of Homeland.

On Good Friday, April 8, 1977, the founding members began to arrive at the center we had manifested. For Treenie and me, it was the realization of a dream that had begun years earlier in Tasmania.

23

Bowled by a Battler

An Aussie battler is a man or woman who battles the odds, finding life a struggle. Australians have a great affection for such people, although the affection fades if the battler overcomes the odds. Then you run into the "tall-poppy" syndrome—but that's another story.

I met a typical Aussie battler at a time when I was feeling a mite uppity. This was before we founded the Homeland commune, during our travels around Oz. I guess we all go through such stages, when arrogance blinds us to the fact we have a lot to learn. Generally, however, life provides the perfect opportunity or person to teach us about humility.

Being a Nature lover, I had quite a large collection of potted plants, most of which I either sold or gave away when we left Tasmania to travel. Because I was attached to them, however, I put my collection of insectivorous plants in a glass container and took them with us. Each time we stopped at a trailer park, I put the container of plants in the sun on the trailer's drawbar.

One day, well into our travels, we stopped at a particularly shady park in Coffs Harbour, so I carried the plants around our trailer looking for a patch of sunlight. As I finally placed them in an acceptable spot, a short, balding man in his sixties approached me, staring wide-eyed at the plants.

This was long enough ago that the Venus's-fly-trap with its bright red, teeth-lined jaws was quite a novelty in Oz, a real eye-catcher. That, along with glistening sundews, and a few sprawling purple pitcher plants, all made for a fairly bizarre collection. Hence my attachment. In fact, I still have them.

"Gawd, mate! I ain't never seen nuffink like them!"

He sounded like a Cockney just plucked from the sound of Bow Bells, his voice squeezed out with lemon. (Cockneys are born within the sound of Bow Bells Church in London.) It was obvious to me that he was uneducated. This was not to be one of my better moments. Feelings of superiority surged in me as I proudly instructed him about the plants. I told him how they grew, and how they had adapted different methods for catching insects.

He listened intently, making just enough response to confirm his ignorance and to keep my ego well inflated. When I had about exhausted my knowledge of the plants, overwhelming him with common and botanical names, I was acutely aware that he could probably remember nothing, yet he made no move to depart.

"Watcha doing then, mate? You live 'ere?"

It was not a dumb question, even though ours was obviously a small traveling trailer, for many trailer owners were residents. I filled him in on just how and why we were there. Again, he listened carefully, nodding his head vigorously in obvious admiration.

"How long have you lived in Australia?" I asked.

"Thirty-five years, mate. Ain't lost none of the ole lingo, 'ave I?" He was inordinately proud of his accent.

142

And then it all unfolded. Life kicked me in the belly, deflating my wind as the man told me just a bit of *his* story.

"Me and the missus live 'ere now. We luv it. This park's the best place we've ever lived. Ten months ago, I was an alcoholic. I suppose I allus will be, but I mean I was drinking then. I'd been drinking on and orf for twenty years, wastin' me money on booze and smokes. Smoked forty fags a day since Gawd knows when."

He paused, staring at me nervously. I think he half expected me to tell him to get lost.

"Any'ow, ten months ago I says to Ada, after a really bad booze-up, 'That's it gal. I've about 'ad it. If I don't do sumfink real soon, I'm gonna be a gonner. And then what'll 'appen to you?'"

He stared me in the eye. "Know what? I sold me little old shack of an 'ouse we lived in, paid off all me booze debts, bought a car and trailer, and drove us from Sydney to 'ere. We fell in luv with the place, and bin 'ere ever since." Stretching to his full, meager height, he continued proudly. "Know what? From the day I sold our 'ouse, I've never agin 'ad any booze or touched a fag. 'Ow's that?"

Without ever realizing it, this man had cut me down to size. I now saw him as a human being of equal status, a person I now viewed without prejudice or judgment, and with respect.

"I think that's incredible." I took his hand and shook it warmly. "Listening to your story has humbled me." And I meant it! "I thought I had been pretty clever overcoming the obstacles I've faced in the last few months, along with a few personal fears, but compared with you, my achievements are less than nothing."

We sat in the sun and chatted for quite a while, man to man, and I saw even more deeply just how much he had accomplished. He had sold his house, got rid of all the furniture, changed his life-style, renewed and rekindled hope in his wife who had stuck with him, *and* stopped a lifetime habit of alcohol and cigarettes — all in one go.

He was truly a simple man. I suspect that he succeeded against the odds because he was not smart enough to know the overwhelming odds against him. He taught me to be humble enough for life to reach me; he taught me that judging others only reveals our own arrogance.

24

The Concrete Blues

A few hundred miles north of Coffs Harbour on the East Coast of Oz, I had yet another trailer park encounter. When we arrived at this park, I was handicapped in setting up camp by a poisoned hand. About a week previously, we had camped for two glorious weeks at Noosa Heads. I was gutting and cleaning fish that Duncan and Adrian were catching, when a fish spine jabbed me in the hand. Harmless bream, would you believe! Everybody knows that the spines of a bream are not laced with poison, but despite that, I had a badly swollen, throbbing hand, patterned with strange fiery marks across the palm. Treenie had nagged me to go to a doctor, but a week had passed and I was still reluctant, my philosophy at that stage being never go to a doctor while you are still breathing.

So it was that at this trailer park I met a retired man in his sixties with an eager, friendly manner, obviously craving someone to talk to.

Once I accepted his friendly overtures, he talked for three hours nonstop about his chief passion in life — concrete! And I do mean passion. He had been an engineer, building bridges and dams all over the world. He was consumed by his love for concrete. I cannot recall a time before or since when I have been so totally bored.

We sat on a bench in the blazing hot sun, my bound

hand throbbing, heat dancing in hazy waves around us, and I had the fight of my life just keeping my eyes open. There were times when I drifted away, staring at him through glazed, unfocused eyes, waiting in vain for the torrential outpouring of words to cease. Such was the man's enthusiasm that his voice rose several decibels, his words proceeding with all the energy of some of those rivers he must have dammed. I heard all there was to hear about grades and mixes of concrete, the when, how, and why of every mix ever known. All this information went in one ear, rattled around, then fell out the other.

When, after three of the longest, hottest, most stupefying hours of my entire life, he suddenly paused, caught his breath, and asked me what was wrong with my hand, I was completely unprepared.

Battling my way through a fog of exhaustion, of sheer concrete boredom, I gaped at him stupidly as I struggled to catch up. "Oh! What? Ah—my hand? Oh, yes—it's poisoned."

"How did that happen?" he asked kindly.

So I told him the whole sorry story in great detail.

"Come with me," he offered. "My wife has an old-fashioned concoction that might fix it for you." With that, he jumped to his feet and strode briskly away, rather as though we had just finished a five-minute chat. I lurched to my feet and followed.

When we reached his van, my mind still churning like a concrete mixer, his wife examined my hand with motherly concern and care. She eyed me with what I took as sympathy when her husband told her we had been chatting for a *little* while. "I reckon this Bascilicon ointment will heal it," she said, producing a flat tin of what appeared to be thick tar.

Plastering the gooey mix all over my hand, she rebandaged it. "Now, see how you go," she said with great concern. "I'm sure that ointment will do the trick. It'll draw out the poison in no time."

Would you believe it, the next morning when I unwrapped my hand, the inflammation and the red streaks of poison had vanished, along with most of the swelling. I was relieved and delighted. I even braved the concrete man to tell his wife what a wonderful lady she was.

It seems a very roundabout way of getting healed, but I was not the only one needing attention. By listening, or trying to listen, to a lonely man talk about his lifelong passion for concrete, I gave myself to him. In turn, his wife gave to me. We both received the appropriate healing. Definitely a good trade, all things considered.

25

Pardon, I Can't Listen

How good are you at listening? I wasn't always very good at it. I could hear, but not really listen. Listening is about attention; hearing is about ears. Even as I type these words, I can hear workmen digging up some nearby drains, but I am not listening to them. I hear the sound of voices, the sound of work, all sounds that my ears are compelled to receive. I say this to emphasize the difference between listening as an active participant, and uninvolved hearing.

When Treenie and I farmed in Tasmania, our working day began at 5:00 A.M. and if we were lucky ended by around 7:00 P.M. Except, of course, at hay time, calving time, and other peak periods. All that work and our unpaid bills placed a lot of pressure on me. Most of the time I was preoccupied, physically and mentally, so I did not have as much time for the children as I would have liked. On far too many occasions, I remember Duncan or Adrian tugging at my sleeve, trying to get my attention. "Dad. Dad, you're not listening," they would say. And I replied, "Yes, I am; I can hear you."

We were both right, but they were far more right than I. I could, indeed, hear them, but I was not listening. I did not know *how* to listen. I didn't even know that listening was different from hearing. Unintentionally, I had learned how not to listen at school. The teachers were so dull, so ploddingly unimaginative, I used to tune them out. Not listening to them allowed me time for daydreaming, which helped me retain my sanity. I could, however, *hear* the teacher's voice as a monotonous drone in the background.

I confess, I was in my midforties when I finally began to understand what listening really entailed. One of the indicators came when I gave a lecture to a group of people in Brisbane, capital of Queensland. After my talk, several enthusiastic people approached me.

"Michael, I didn't realize that you are a follower of Krishnamurti," said one. (I am not, though I have read one of his books.)

"Gee, it was really nice to hear you speaking from such a Christian background. What church do you attend?" asked another. (I no longer attend church. I prefer a direct line of communication!)

"Michael, you trickster! You didn't tell us you were going to speak from the *Course of Miracles*," a friend said. (I did not. I have never read the *Course of Miracles* or attended any of their workshops.)

"The yogic influence is very strong in you," said a stranger, "even though it is mixed and mingled with the Tao." (I know very little about yoga, and as with the way of Tao, can only respect each for what it has to offer.)

"You have obviously had neurolinguistic training," another stranger said. (This was the first time I had ever heard of it!)

I was thoughtful when I returned home that evening. How was it that each of these people had heard a quite different philosophy in my words? I spoke, as always, only from my own experience, my life and living, and nothing else. I came to realize that those people who had spoken to me after my lecture had heard me through the framework of their own philosophies or beliefs. Basically, all that I said was mentally translated into a format that they could find acceptable and familiar. I call this secondhand hearing. And, I saw as well, I did exactly the same thing when I "listened" to a speaker.

That experience was a turning point for me. I finally learned that listening is an active participation, something involving the power of the moment, and the power and purpose of the participants.

Treenie also had a turning point around listening. I suspect that unless we are trained to listen, we all have that special moment when aware listening draws us closer to the communicator. And, sadly, there are those who never learn to listen. It does require a certain humility, and we humans are inclined to be short on that.

For Treenie, it happened while we were living at the Homeland commune. She was very involved in the office work, in the day-to-day management, in being a wife, in personal growth, and in being a mother. But she was so busy it was increasingly difficult for the children to gain her attention. You know how it is: "Mum, Mum, Mum, MUM," on and on, until they get the desired results. However, one day it changed.

Instead of chanting the usual "Mum, Mum," Adrian said, "Treenie," and had her immediate attention. Treenie was shocked. In that moment, she realized that the children were part of the backdrop of sound she did not really listen to. The people she listened to were people who called her Treenie!

As Adrian succinctly explained it, "You listen to the adults, but you hardly ever hear us kids." Now, as the father of my two darling granddaughters, he will have to learn the same lesson.

The power of listening is very simple. If we listen to a child, a river, music, a waterfall, or fountain, whatever— if we really listen—then we are fully in the moment and vitally connected with the power of life, which is the power of the moment. Listening links us with "now power." It opens us to discovery. It opens each of us to a brand new relationship with other people, with ourself, and with life. And all we need do is *really* listen. Try it. It sure is simple, but powerful enough to transform your life.

26
Terms of Embarrassment

When in the 1970s I discovered that a certain way of thinking or relating to life was termed "alternative," I was truly puzzled. I still am. How can a person's desire for green forests; clean, breathable air; drinkable water; pure, healthy food; and peace possibly be an alternative? Alternative to what—eroded soil, polluted air, contaminated water, food laced with chemical additives, and war? Is this now accepted as normal?

I went through an angry stage over these issues, but that has passed. My commitment to inner growth and expanded awareness mercifully carried me through and beyond my emotional anger. For me, the so-called alternatives of today are, in fact, the appropriates of tomorrow. And tomorrow has arrived! I am convinced that protecting the forests, helping produce clean air, pure water, and healthy food, and desiring world peace, are appropriate. Any other thinking is radically alternative.

When Treenie and I were at the height of our inner change, we were very enthusiastic about our new way of thinking. Some people called it "New Age" thinking, and I can relate to this. Whereas I am not sure that anything is truly "new," that designation points to the difference between old and new ways of expression. For me, the old expression relates to life in terms of separation and blame, while the new embraces wholeness and responsibility. This philosophy offers no conflict with religious thought, but provides a way to live a chosen religion. If you consider the implications, you find vast differences between these two sometimes overlapping streams of human expression.

Treenie and I often verbalized our enthusiasm for the way of wholeness and responsibility in conversations with friends. Some found it acceptable, even desirable; some were threatened. Imagine not being able to blame someone else, or the government, for your personal misfortunes!

When we were about to leave Tasmania on our travels, I eyed all the empty space on the white sides of our newly acquired Nissan E20, a large, vanlike vehicle. With Treenie's approval, I asked David, an organic gardening friend from Hobart—and a sign painter—if he would indulge us with his skills. With some amusement, he wrote in large bold letters, UNFOLD LIKE A FLOWER, along one side and, ENTER A NEW AGE, along the other. He painted, LOVE, on the back door, and with a flourish, the vehicle's name across the front, LOVE BUG. We were ready to face the world!

Before I drove down to the local township, I planned my strategy. Let's face it, to drive a vehicle like Love Bug into a township where everyone believed after ten years they really knew you is to invite embarrassment. Life, however, had taught me a lesson about embarrassment that I intended to apply. We'd learned that lesson during our years of change, when Treenie and I were visited with ever-increasing numbers of New Age people. Maybe word had gone out on the network, but travelers from mainland Oz seemed to find us easily on our remote southern island.

On this particular morning, I was on my way to the kitchen. As I passed our bathroom, I saw the door was wide open, the shower curtain drawn back, and a dripping wet and naked Jane stood in full view under the shower. She had dropped in on us the previous day. "Hi, Mike," she called out.

I stopped, stared in astonishment at her, turned bright red with embarrassment, and continued on to the kitchen. As I sipped a cup of coffee, I tried to sort out my emotions. I was embarrassed. Why should I be embarrassed? I was fully clothed, in my own house, doing what I should be doing, yet I was mortified. Jane had stood stark naked in front of me, and she was not the least bit embarrassed. It did not make sense.

Gradually, I figured it out. Had Jane tried to quickly draw the shower curtain, or to cover herself with a towel, or had she demonstrated some embarrassment, then I would not have. In other words, because she was not embarrassed, I took it on. Because of my conditioning, one of us had to. It was the confrontation of an extreme, not the nudity, that had embarrassed me.

Remembering all this, I realized that Love Bug was now the extreme, and I was ready for a practice run in the confrontation of embarrassment. If I failed, then I was going to have a very difficult time as we traveled around. Accordingly, I drove Love Bug down to the township, and pulled up with the words UNFOLD LIKE A FLOWER directly facing Snowy, the owner of a local garage, and one of the straightest and most conservative men I knew. As it happened, he was pumping gas out in front, so my timing was perfect. I walked over to him, looked him directly in the eyes, and asked, "Well, Snowy, what do you think of that?"

Snowy's jaw fell open. He snapped it shut while the bright red color of embarrassment swept up over his face, disappearing into his snowy white hair. I admit, I'm glad I did not know what he was thinking. Without a word, he spun around and stomped off into his workshop.

It worked. By directly confronting him, I had transferred to him what should have been my embarrassment.

Of course, traveling around Oz applying my strategy with so much success, I began to think I was invincible. Time for another lesson.

We were on the West Coast when I met my match. In fact, it was no contest! It was midmorning, and we were playing a Jim Reeves tape, one of his sweet and slow themes on love. Suddenly, shattering the mood, there was a loud knocking on the door.

A large and formidable woman filled the doorway to overflowing. Her voice, as she clambered in was even larger.

"Hallelujah! Hallelujah! I just knew there had to be some God-loving folks in here!" And with that as an introduction, she launched into the most full-on bible bash I had ever encountered. She annihilated me, not only meeting me eye-to-eye, but thrusting her beaming face into mine.

It was such an overwhelming confrontation that I backed away, while she followed me into the trailer and sat firmly down, fully prepared to convert us to her mode of Christianity.

So, simple as the confrontational effect may be, be careful. Someone else may do it better.

❀   ❀   ❀

The kids were not embarrassed with Love Bug while we were traveling, but when we settled down it was a whole new ball game. They were now with people they would see tomorrow, and all the tomorrows to follow. What would the other kids at school think? Now, *that* was embarrassing. It was bad enough for it to be known they lived in a commune, but the Love Bug as well—that was just too much.

To comply with their request, Treenie or I would drop them off just outside Bellingen, so nobody associated them with our vehicle. Things got even worse for them when the local school kids dubbed Love Bug the Pansy Wagon! Personally, I thought it was rather creative, even if the flower connotation was somewhat oblique.

The children dealt with it, each in his or her own way. I think Tracy was the first one to not care what the other kids thought, but Adrian's approach was both smart and simple.

Treenie and I were driving past the tennis courts one afternoon, as some of the school kids, Adrian among them, were practicing at the nets. As instructed, we did not wave, and then we heard Adrian call out in a loud, jeering voice, "Hippy freaks, hippy freaks!" before turning away from us and continuing to play tennis.

Later on, he told us that after jeering at us, he said to all the other kids, "That was my mum and dad." Of course, they did not take him seriously. From that time on, he never again had to pretend about us, or about Love Bug. They just did not believe him!

27

The Price

Without doubt, life is our everyday teacher, but sometimes it becomes downright sneaky. Without warning, we are plunged into a lesson where the real issue is so disguised, so subtle, that we are left floundering. Yet there are moments when a sudden insight, a flash of inspired genius, or even a dream reveals the answer that can bail us out.

When I began my career as a writer, I found it tough going. I tried to combine being an organic farming consultant with being a writer, and the writing suffered. Then life organized a nationwide drought in Oz. To economize, my various farming clients cut out their consultant. Not their smartest move, but it gave my writing career the required nudge. In retrospect, the first year of writing did nothing more than extract all the negative nonsense from my system, so I produced and destroyed two manuscripts of quite clever rubbish. Then I settled down to write.

I was still involved in the mental-purge stage when the rains came, but I kept on writing, never again taking up the consultancy. However, my writing and a decent income did not equate. I was at that stage where a writer is paying his or her dues, which really means collecting an ever-growing pile of rejection slips. It has been said that you need to suffer to be a good writer. For the life of me, I don't see how you can become a published writer without suffering, especially if you have the audacity to think you are even halfway good, or are at all attached to the words you write.

So you will understand that when I was offered the opportunity to write the biography of a person unknown to me, I jumped at the chance. Money, I drooled; I just might get paid. Even Treenie enjoyed such potent speculation!

From the beginning, the whole assignment had a touch of mystery. I knew the subject was a man, but I was given no name, and the address was in a very remote location a fair drive from where I lived. An arrangement was made for me to meet the man at his home.

At the appointed date, I headed off happily in my car. I found the right township, and following directions, wended my way deeper and deeper into a remote network of hills and valleys. As I drove, I fantasized about what my subject's occupation might have been, for I had learned he was now retired. Let him be the retired curator of some famous botanical gardens, I thought, or an international landscape designer. Perhaps I will have to travel extensively to research his work—Europe maybe, or. . . . On and on went my thoughts, as I followed the very narrow lane.

Finally, I reached my destination. I pulled into the drive of an older-style timber home. A man stood by the door as though expecting me.

"Er—Mr. White?" I called, as I got out of the car.

"Chubby! Call me Chubby," he bellowed, while I stared at him in mild amazement. Talk about appropriate—the man was about five feet tall, and about five feet wide. He didn't walk toward me; he ran in a waddling gait of enormous energy and vitality, radiating warmth and friendliness. When we met, I offered my hand, but he waded past it to envelop me in a vast bear hug. Having lived in a commune, I was well into hugging, but this one took me off guard. Probably I like to know the huggee first. Not that I could have hugged him back even if I wanted to, since my arms were trapped under his.

Then a curious thing happened. As he released me and stepped back, I experienced one of the most powerful jolts of rapport I have felt with another human being. And he felt it, too. The empathy between us was so strong it was as though I was inside him, with him, knowing him — yet we had only just met.

In silent astonishment, I listened and watched while this character introduced me to his seventh wife, a real knockout, at least forty years his junior; his twelfth child, a lovely boy; and showed me the faint scars of his fourth face lift! During most of this, I was practically speechless, wondering what I had let myself in for. Everything that Chubby did was accompanied by his exuberant energy. When, on his invitation, I followed him through the house and out onto the veranda, he gestured to a comfortable seat for me to take. I remained standing, admiring the view, but he leaped into the air and went crashing into his chair with a shock that reverberated through the entire house.

"Well, Mike," he boomed, "I suppose you'll be wanting to know what I did for a living." He eyed me speculatively. "Sit down, sit down," he commanded, pointing to the chair opposite him.

161

I shook my head. "I'll stand for a while. I've just had a long session in the car."

Chubby looked me straight in the eye. "Well, I'll tell you. I'm a retired gangster. I spent the last fifteen years as a bagman."

I sat, collapsing into the chair as though shot. My voice, when it emerged, was a pathetic squeak. "Er—what's a bagman?"

He told me that a bagman collects money from various shady businesses to pay the police for turning a blind eye to their illegal operations. For the next two hours, I listened to a nonstop outline of Chubby's life story. He did not mention names, but he told me the most horrendous saga of a misspent life I had ever heard. As a child, he had been trained to steal at the orphanage where he was caged—not housed, not homed, but caged. He and the other children there were sexually abused and regularly beaten. They were degraded and criminalized, and, as would be expected, many of them became products of their training and conditioning.

Chubby had been a gangster and nightclub owner. He had dealt in prostitution and drugs, in thieving and violence all his life. It was all he knew. As he told me this, he ripped his shirt up from his huge belly and showed me the puckered scars of several stab wounds, and one on his chest where a bullet had entered his body. Not for one moment did his voice drop a decibel under an enthusiastic bellow, as he continued to detail one awful episode after another.

He told me about his moral code, something he was proud of. When young girls trying to get into prostitution came into his club, he had them brought into his office. If they were under *his* acceptable age, he treated them to a meal. While they were eating, he arranged for one of the welfare groups to pick the girls up as they left the club. According to him, they numbered several hundred girls barely into their teens, and plenty younger than teenagers. Apparently most of them were persuaded to return home.

As Chubby spoke, my thoughts drifted. What in the name of wonderment am I doing here? Is this for real? Do they have "Candid Camera" in Oz? How do I extricate myself from this one? Boy, Michael, you're really done it this time! Could I possibly write his story? Yes, I could, because of this weird empathy between us. Empathy with a gangster! My God, what next?

"So what do you think?" he asked abruptly.

"Would you mind repeating that last bit," I said.

Finally, he launched into an impassioned plea for me to write his biography, while I tried to figure a way out. Suddenly, like a ray of sunshine, that moment of inspired genius came to the surface, and I grabbed on with both hands.

"I understand you were told that I'm an established author," I said mildly.

"Yes. Yes, I was," he nodded vigorously.

"Well, I'm afraid it's not true," I said, trying not to look smug. "I have written a book, but just a little book. It's nothing that someone like you would even notice."

"What was it about?" he asked, disappointment clear on his face.

"It was a gardening book." I spoke the word "gardening" as though it epitomized the absolute pits in subject matter.

He looked deflated. "What's it called?"

I was feeling pleased by now, sensing a quick victory. "A *Guide to Organic Gardening in Australia*," I replied.

Chubby stared past me, his eyes bulging. His face transformed as though he had seen *the* light, or heard *the* word. He came out of his deep recliner as if ejected, and I swear his feet were running before they touched down.

"Sweetie! Sweetie!" he bellowed, bolting off the veranda and dashing into the house. "It's *him*, it's *him!*"

By now I, too, had jumped to my feet and was staring anxiously around me. I knew that this was Chubby's retirement hideaway and that several past associates would be happy to know where he was. For a moment I thought Chubby had caught sight of such a gentlemen. Perhaps someone hoping to improve the ventilation in Chubby's chest, or offer some immediate and violent surgery—but there was nobody in sight.

Bewildered, I followed Chubby's passage down the hall, and peered cautiously into the kitchen. Sweetie smiled at me as though I were a miracle of the risen dead. My bewilderment was not improved when Chubby jabbed a finger in my direction, rushed over, and to my consternation, once again embraced me, but with greatly increased fervor.

"It's him! It's him," he bellowed in my ear.

By now, I had caught on. I realized that "him" was in fact me.

"What," I managed to croak, "have I done?"

In a stentorian bellow, Chubby told me that he and

Sweetie had recently visited another "retired associate" even farther up the valley. To their surprise, they found a magnificent garden of flowers, shrubs, trees, and vegetables there, all growing organically. How had the friend learned to produce such a magnificent display?

"It's easy," he told them. "I just bought a book called *A Guide to Organic Gardening in Australia,* and followed it. It's so simple to understand even I could do it."

Clever me, I thought.

"You *will* write my book, Mike; I know it," Chubby said. "You were sent by God to do it."

Numbed by the sudden turn of events, my inspiration in shreds, I retreated to the veranda.

There was only one route left to go, so over drinks I confronted Chubby directly. "I can't do it, Chubby. I don't have the skills you need and I wouldn't even know how to begin."

Before the words were even out of my mouth, Chubby was waving his arms around to stop them. "You *can* do it," he bellowed. "You *must* do it. The books will be an exposé on all the corruption I've been involved in."

"*Books,*" I gasped. "Books, as in more than one?"

"Of course. There will be two books. The first up until I was twenty-five years old, and the second covering the rest of my life. You will need to meet my ex-associates. They can verify my story; they can show you the inside of the rackets and the corruption I was involved in."

"This is absolutely ridiculous," I burst out. "Putting me among people like that would be like putting a lamb among a pack of wolves. I don't have the right aptitude for this. I would be an innocent among the corrupted."

"I know! I know! That's what I want. That's the way it should be. You wouldn't be biased. Think of all the young and innocent girls you could save from corruption. It would be honest if you wrote it. It must be honest." He eyed me calculatingly. "Think of those poor girls I told you about. If you write an honest book, it could help others like them."

"Why this sudden desire for honesty?" I asked. "You've lived dishonestly all your life. Why be honest now? What difference will it make? Why not write the books yourself and lie all you like. You must surely be good at it!" I was getting bold.

An expression of profound shock transformed Chubby's face, and to my utter surprise, he began to cry. Tears streamed in a copious flow down his puffy cheeks. "My mother went to her deathbed believing I was a liar," he wept, "and I *never* lied to her. I might have cheated her once or twice and maybe stole a few things, but I never, never lied to her." His shoulders shook as the passion of his indignation overflowed.

I was almost beyond shock by now, and beginning to feel that I definitely held the upper hand. "I'm sorry, Chubby. If you want honesty, I honestly don't think I can do it. Much as it disturbs me to think about people like you corrupting young girls, it is way, way out of my area of expertise. I don't have the skills to interrogate and extract the sort of information that I'd need." I smiled sympathetically.

"I'll pay you $20,000 to write it. Half in advance the moment you say you'll do it. Plus I'll give you fifty percent of the film rights and a generous royalty on each book sold."

The tears had magically disappeared. With a shrewd look, he watched my reaction.

I gulped. I was broke, and I mean broke. "I'll think about it," I fenced, visions of an immediate $10,000 floating in my imagination like water lilies in a pond.

With difficulty, I pried myself away from Chubby, his energy, his exuberance, his arms, and finally from his house. At my car, he gave me another farewell bear hug, just as a farmyard duck waddled past. Deceptively fast, Chubby bent over and grabbed the duck, all in one smooth flurry of motion.

"Here you are, Mike. You take this duck to seal our friendship," he said in complete sincerity, thrusting it into my unresisting arms. My brain was about half a minute behind the action. In a daze, I took the duck, climbed in the car, and backed out of the driveway. As I drove away, the duck looked at me pensively, opened its beak, and said what we both knew, "Quack."

"You're right," I replied. "I'm quackers!"

It took me well over an hour to tell the story to Treenie. When I finished and described the very lucrative money offer, I asked, "So how do you feel about it? Ten thousand dollars would be very handy."

"No." Treenie was adamant. "Definitely no. I am not having you mixed up with criminals and gangsters. I don't care how much money he's offered you."

"Gee, I'm glad you've kept an open mind," I mocked.

I refused to make a quick decision, but during the next few days all my instincts were to reject the offer. Finally, I decided to decline. As I crossed the garden heading indoors to write Chubby a letter, my back suddenly gave way, and I collapsed. I was laid up with one of my periodic spells of back pain, although it improved fairly quickly. However, while flat on my back for those few days, I could not help but think that my back had effectively prevented me from writing the letter to Chubby. So I gave the matter further consideration.

I began to think maybe I should write the books after all. Perhaps a book that revealed Chubby's connection as a bagman with the police might do some good. Possibly it would expose police corruption; that ought to do some good. The more I thought about it, the more convinced I became that good could come of my writing these books.

I thought about the money, uncovering a disconcerting memory. Only a week or so before this whole episode began, I had told a friend that I could not be bought. He believed that everyone had his or her price. I had been adamant that I did not. Was I now about to be bought for $20,000? I looked honestly into myself, into my own integrity. No, it was not the money. All this rethinking had come after I decided to reject the offer, and then life had clobbered me. Was life indicating that I should go ahead?

That night, I had a dream. While realistic and vivid dreams are part of my life, this one was very strange. I dreamed about the Devil. I never dream about devils, I don't even believe in them. However, in this dream, the Devil was talking to someone or something I could not see. It was as though I was accidently overhearing the Devil.

What made it all the more peculiar was that I was wide awake during this dream, my eyes open to the morning daylight. However, I heard the Devil clearly, and it was quite a revelation.

"This sucker says he cannot be bought," the Devil said, "and looking into him, he is right as far as money is concerned. But every sucker has his price. You know this fool's price? Let him believe that he is doing 'good'—that's his price. Every sucker has his price. I'll divert him from his true and chosen path. I'll lead him on a 'do-good' crusade."

I sat bolt upright in shock, the words echoing in my head as though they had been spoken aloud. Although I did not have a clue what my chosen path was, in that moment I knew with absolute certainty what it was not.

I got out of bed, showered and dressed, and then I wrote to Chubby politely turning down his offer. I wished him luck when the *real* writer came along. As I wrote, I glanced around me. "Okay, Devil," I said softly, "last time you hit me in the back. If you want to stop me this time you're going to have to hit me on top of my head—right about now." I waited, not believing it would happen. It did not.

One other thing—we did not eat the duck. It became a family pet!

28

Well, Thanks a Lot!

I was a strong, strapping young man at age seventeen, not frightened of work, but given to daydreaming. With my parents, I lived in Trumpington at the time, a village about twelves miles from our farm. We had a large vegetable garden there, and one day I stayed home to dig it the old-fashioned way, with a spade—the only way then, I might add.

I enjoyed digging. It was a rhythmic action, rather like physical poetry, and I found it deeply satisfying. In the first quarter of an hour, a graceful, repetitive motion would catch me and I could then turn the soil hour after hour with scarcely a break, so sustaining was the flow of energy. The spade and I became one in this age-old action. And I found the contact with the sweet-smelling earth stimulating, the sight of fresh-turned soil a constant fascination. So when our retired next-door neighbor, Mr. Allen, popped his head over the garden wall and offered me one pound to dig his vegetable garden, I accepted instantly. I knew I could easily accomplish it in a full day, and one pound was a normal week's wage for me. Dad had no objections, so I took the job.

Two days later back on our farm, I held up the one-pound note to Stan with whom I was working. "You see this?" I said. "I worked damn hard for it. If anyone deserves this more than I do, they can have it." It was one of those brash, foolish statements of youth.

He looked at me thoughtfully, a gleam in his eyes. "Do you remember a week ago at the local shop, seeing that old crippled woman in the wheelchair? She was trying to get in through the doorway as I came out."

"Yes, I remember her. What about it?"

"She deserves that one-pound note more than you do," he said cunningly, "'cos she hasn't got any money. I happen to know that."

"So how do you figure she *deserves* it more than me?"

"'Cos you can work and earn more; she can't."

I stared at him in surprise, my own words echoing in my head. I knew he was right.

"Okay, she can have it. But there's one condition. You've got to give it to her; I'm not."

"Why not?" he asked.

"Because I'd be too embarrassed. I won't do it. Either you give it to her, or I keep it."

He held out his hand. I watched my hard earned one-pound note disappear into his pocket. Me and my big mouth, I thought. I had had it less than a day! But inside, I felt good about it.

Neither of us knew where the old woman lived, so we agreed that Stan would give her the money the next time he saw her in the local shop where they were both regular customers. I told my dad about it on the way home. He gave me an odd sort of look, but said nothing.

Three days later, Stan told me he had seen the crippled woman in the shop the previous afternoon. He had given her the one-pound note, told her the story that went with it, and comforted her when she burst into tears.

"God help me," she wept. "Do you know I've only got one and a half pence to my name?" And she cried some more. She said that she had come into the shop to buy a couple of meager items, not knowing how she would pay for them. The one-pound note was more money in one go than she had seen in over a year.

When I heard all this I felt pretty good. In fact, I felt better than if I had spent the pound on myself.

A few days later, Stan and I looked up from our labors to see the old woman making her way slowly up the long farm drive, pedaling her wheelchair with hands and arms. When she reached us, she introduced herself as Miss May Hazell. She had come to say thank you.

Miss May Hazell proved to be a tough lady from the East End of London. In the course of our getting to know her, she told us she had been a bus conductor during the Second World War, and it was a bomb that left her crippled from the waist down—and angry and embittered.

She was as emotionally crippled as she was physically, but for some perverse reason most of her bitterness, caustic and scathing, was aimed at me. And while she loved me for what I had extended to her, she hated me for the fact that she should need it.

Because of my one-pound note, Stan and his entire family took an interest in May Hazell's welfare, and so also did my dad. Under our collective influence, she found a new home and she got a motorized wheelchair. I suspect Dad paid for that. My contribution was to buy her a ton of coal each winter to keep her warm.

When Treenie and I got married, May Hazell often called in. She adored Treenie, but still treated me like dirt. It got so bad, it became a joke. Strangely, I was not particularly hurt by her considerable spite toward me. Her thinking did not exactly command my respect. She was a member of the Salvation Army, and while I have nothing but admiration for all they stand for, she was not their greatest example of stalwart love!

One afternoon she was ranting about how she hated the rockets "they" were sending to the moon. (She meant the wicked Americans.) "Rockets are the Devil's work," she said.

"Oh, why?" I asked mildly.

She turned on me with her customary anger. "Because they will make holes in heaven as they rip through on their way to the moon. All the good people will fall out and be killed all over again. I tell you, it's the Devil's work!"

What could I say?

After one particular visit, when I had copped a tongue-lashing unusual in its vitriolic fervor even for her, I turned to Treenie. "Why do I bother with her?" I asked. "Why don't I just tell her to go to hell?"

I tell you, Treenie was special from the moment of birth. She put her arms around me, saying, "My darling, you put up with her and continue to help her because you are showing yourself your greater virtues. You do it because you care, not because you need her approval or friendship."

I looked at her skeptically, but she was perfectly serious. Later, when I thought about it, I realized that her insight was remarkably accurate. I continued to help May Hazell, regardless of how she treated me, because I had uncovered a deep streak of compassion within myself.

At this impressionable age, I suspect that if May Hazell had told me how kind and wonderful I was with the same vigor that she scorned and rejected me, I could have become hooked on praise.

Her rejection took me deeper into myself, beyond the deceit of conceit, revealing a deep core of compassion based on a love for humanity, rather than the attraction of personalities. The gift she offered me was simple, but it was a hidden gift. Finding it revealed my power, for our real power lies within compassion and love.

29

In Harmony With Nature

In general, humanity has developed away from Nature. We have become aggressors, seeking to dominate and subdue the Nature that surrounds us, rather than integrate with it. Of course, now that humans are becoming environmentally threatened, we are seeking to make changes in our attitude and approach; even so, our change is laced with skepticism and reluctance. As a species, we react aggressively rather than respond intelligently. I suspect that in the changes we have induced, this more than anything is the lesson we have to learn: to apply ourselves to the issues we now confront intelligently and without fear.

When I farmed in Tasmania, I became one of the leading organic farmers in that state, and I learned about cynicism first hand. About fifteen years ago on appearances to promote my first book, *A Guide to Organic Gardening in Australia,* I was often introduced as the "alternative" gardener with the radical ideas. Can you imagine that? However, two years ago, publicizing the book's rewritten, enlarged, and updated version, *The Natural Magic of Mulch,* it was taken for granted that any intelligent person knew organic gardening was the only way to go.

In my early days as an organic farmer, I was acutely aware of how much I needed to learn. I read most of the books on the subject, certainly the classics, but so often they had little application to my hill property in Tasmania. I watched as my cows, standing in lush, improved pasture, stretched their necks through the barbed wire fence to crop some of the sparse forest grass and weeds on the other side—and by observation, I learned why. I watched my cows get bloat grazing the new season pasture on a wet night; I pumped the usual syringe full of penicillin into each infected quarter of my milking cows, wondering why mastitis was such a scourge in the dairy herd—and by observation, I learned why. I noticed that despite having a fair number of earthworms in the garden, in the farm soil and pastures they were very rare—and by observation, I learned why. Invariably, simple observation will reveal an answer to an open, inquiring mind. For me, the combination of observation and application became a very powerful tool.

Those earthworms are a wonderful example. I had been working on our highest hills, an area we had bought from the Forestry Department. This area had been cleared of all scrubby growth, but the large trees and a few acre patches of wattle had been left. The new pasture was established, but it was not exactly thriving. It was autumn, and I was harrowing the pasture to spread out the mass of dried cowpats that littered the ground. I had only been around the 180 acres a couple of times, when I stopped for a bite of lunch. The pasture was surrounded by forest on three sides, and as I idled along the edge of the forest and ate, I kicked at a cowpat I had missed. Underneath was a large, fat earthworm. My interest intensified. Half an hour later, I had managed to find three other worms under cowpats on the edge of the forest. I then turned my attention to the pasture, but another half hour failed to reveal a single hidden earthworm.

Instead of resuming harrowing, I sat down in the shade of the forest for a good think. As an aspiring organic farmer, I needed earthworms. Nothing, but nothing, is a greater ally to the organic farmer. I knew that earthworms bred in the wet season, and the Tasmanian wet generally came in the winter. My observation indicated that the earthworms preferred the older, more mature cowpats. I knew that earthworms liked to breed in rich organic matter, so it was a fairly safe bet that old cowpats would qualify. However, I was about to harrow them—break them down and spread them out over the pasture. This happened all over the farm each year, which was good from a fertilizing point of view, but no good from the earthworms' perspective for breeding. It was a routine that left the worms little incentive or inducement to increase their numbers.

Bearing in mind that all farmers harrowed their pasture each autumn, my carefully thought-out decision to withhold harrowing until the spring was both controversial and courageous. Not only did I leave that particular pasture unharrowed, I applied the principle to the whole farm. That first winter, I kept a close eye on the mature cowpats, hoping that earthworms would vindicate my observations. They did. While the breeding program was not spectacular, I found earthworms under a scattering of old cowpats over all the farm. I learned that earthworms lay grayish-white egg capsules, each capsule containing about twenty eggs.

I shared my theory with a few other farmers, and most were skeptical. Surely, one said, if that was the case, all farmers would know about it. When I asked him why he harrowed his pasture each autumn, he admitted it was because all the other farmers did. Besides, his father had done it that way.

Three years later, the soil under our pastures was literally seething with earthworms. The method proved successful beyond anything I had imagined. Basically, I switched autumn pasture harrowing to spring. I waited until the earthworms had left the cowpats, their breeding complete, and had moved back into deeper profiles of soil. I then had to harrow the pasture twice, for the cowpats were quite solid after the winter rains. And of course, they were no longer cowpats; they were a mature compost, a better fertilizer than ever.

When I was invited to speak at a farmers' meeting about organic gardening, the skepticism bordered on hostility. At that meeting, I learned that many farmers are genuinely threatened by change and new thinking. I invited them to come and see for themselves what I had done, rather than take my word for it. Out of the sixteen farmers at the meeting, seven came, and I must say that this is testimony more to my powers of persuasion than to their eagerness to learn.

As we gathered around an area thick with old cowpats, I overheard a couple of farmers remark on what a mess it looked. I knelt down, and taking the edge of a large, double cowpat, asked them to watch carefully. As I lifted it, a few hundred earthworms were instantly evident. We broke open the cowpats, counted a few hundred more worms, and I showed them the egg capsules. They had never seen the egg of an earthworm, had never dreamed such numbers were possible in pastures.

What I demonstrated was simple, nothing more than a system of farming in harmony with Nature, which abundantly met my own needs. The principle I based the system on met the needs of the Whole: soil, worms, environment, and myself. By using common sense and following simple observations, I had harnessed the power of Nature without any expense or effort.

I have given many talks on this theme and related subjects. After one such talk in Oz, I was approached by a farmer who ran a large flock of sheep on a thousand acres of land. Rob's problem was his sheepdogs. He had several trained dogs that had to be kept on chains. The dogs hated it, yelping and barking day and night, which in turn frayed the family nerves. He wanted to know if there was any other way of restraining them, other than on chains or in pens.

I suggested that he educate the dogs. While I accepted that they were undoubtedly well trained, they were not well educated. Rob confessed he did not know what I was talking about. "The problem is," he said, "if I let the dogs off, they run wild. They chase the sheep; they wander for miles and get themselves in trouble. They have to be on the chain, it's the only form of control there is. I don't see how education—however that is possible—can alter anything."

"When you have plenty of time," I said, "and you are

not feeling pressured, take the dogs off the chains and walk them around your boundaries. As you walk, talk to them firmly, simply, and very clearly. Most importantly, think about what you are saying. Tell them that this is the boundary of your property and you don't want them to cross it. Tell them they are to leave your sheep well alone unless you detail them to work. In essence, tell them not to stray or chase sheep. As you walk around, repeat this over and over, slowly and with your full attention. Then, when you get home, don't chain the dogs up. Leave them loose and trust them."

Rob looked at me as though I was mad. "You really think that will work?" he asked.

"Educate them and find out." I said.

About six weeks later, we had a letter from Rob. He had tried what I suggested and, to his great astonishment, it had worked. The dogs were free, they did not stray or chase sheep, and of course they no longer barked their frustration and misery. He said that he had never heard of anything quite like it. It had never occurred to him simply to talk to his dogs and tell them exactly what he wanted.

He had not realized that simple is powerful!

It works in other ways, such as in simple cooperation with Nature. When Treenie and I lived in Bellingen, I grew vegetables in the garden during autumn, winter, and spring. Summers were generally too hot and humid. In the first year, when in late winter I went to pick some brussels sprouts, I found they were partly eaten. So were the cabbage heads, and the green shoots of broccoli. After a bit of observation, I discovered the female bower birds were the culprit. It seemed that in very early spring, probably when they were carrying eggs, they looked for green food nourishment. They wiped out my crops that first season.

Next season, I asked the bower birds if we could come to an arrangement. I would leave all the chickweed in the garden—a shallow-rooted, sweet-leafed weed—which they could have, and they could have the large, slightly coarse, outer leaves of cabbage, brussels sprouts, and broccoli, but the hearts of the plants were for my family.

Very early the next spring, the female bower birds first ate the chickweed, then the outer Brussels sprout leaves, then the outer cabbage and broccoli leaves. I harvested all that I had planted for us. To see the outer leaves of brussels sprouts shredded, with the tender heart still intact, is quite extraordinary.

❀   ❀   ❀

If all this sounds fanciful, try it. Nothing is more fruitless than a closed, cynical human. I know, I met one. All those years ago, when the earthworms had become established on our farm, I noticed a new and very welcome phenomenon. The brown-hair stomach worms that commonly parasitized cattle were gradually disappearing from my herd. After a few years of this observation, I understood what was happening. Parasite worm eggs were ejected with the cattle manure onto the pasture. An ever-increasing population of earthworms were eating an ever-decreasing cycle of parasite worm eggs. Eventually, I sold about a dozen cows that were always infested, obviously hosts for the worms, and my days of regularly drenching cattle were at an end.

When, with a small deputation of organic farmers, I approached the then-minister for agriculture in Tasmania to share with him this revelation in grazing, I was jeered at and scorned by that closed, cynical man. He told me that my notion was both fanciful and ridiculous. Not being very tactful, I then told him a few things. The meeting came to a very abrupt end.

Incidents of harmony with Nature are neither rare nor fanciful, but often people are not prepared to talk about them for fear of ridicule.

Lance Rose, my landlord when we lived in Bellingen, has one such story. Lance has been a bushman for most of his life, spending many years cutting down the trees that he would now rather see conserved.

This story concerns a time, long ago, in his woodcutting days. He told it to me shyly, knowing that I would not mock him, yet hesitant about sharing something that might generally be dismissed or rejected.

With a couple of other men, he had been cutting cedar on the higher slopes of McGrath's Hump, a low, forest-covered mountain range near his home. In a steep gully, he scrambled toward the last known stand of cedars on the Hump around midafternoon, and started his chain saw. His mates were still lingering farther down the slope when Lance approached the largest tree. With a sense of shock, very clearly in his head, he heard: *You have finished. Leave us in peace.* Lance was so surprised, he stopped the chain saw and sat down by himself.

By the time his mates were clambering up the slope to join him, he was walking back down.

"What about those last few trees?" they asked.

"I don't think we'll bother to get them," Lance replied. "They're in a steep gully, a real cow of a place to work. Besides, let them stay for seed trees. We've done enough here."

The men shrugged, dismissing the last, small stand of cedar trees. They were forgotten, and continued to grow and thrive unmolested on those remote, densely forested slopes.

Many years later, Lance and his wife, Enid, had a new house built. Lance can now sit by his front door in his favorite chair and, with a pair of binoculars, watch those same favored cedars high up in their dense forest home.

Can you imagine how he must have felt when only a few years ago those cedar trees were rediscovered and hailed as a real find — to be totally protected. There is now a faint, rough walking trail that people can use to see an ancient species of trees that once covered many thousands of square miles of Oz.

It helps when a man is simple enough to be open to the spirit of Nature.

30

Something to Chew On

To thine own self be true. Time-honored words, but how many of us really accept their challenge? How many of us hasten to justify our truth, how many need the acceptance and approval of peers? How many of us can take a stand against the opinions of others and not be threatened or overwhelmed?

Over a decade and a half ago, in my early days of public speaking, my subject was organic farming and gardening. Gradually, however, as my interest in Nature deepened, I began to speak on reconnecting with Nature, treading a delicate balance between the tangible physical Nature surrounding us, and the more intangible Nature that eludes our five senses.

My experiences and suggestions were invariably enthusiastically received. After a talk, a group would form around me, asking questions or sharing personal experiences. I could almost guarantee one particular question: "Michael, are you a vegetarian?"

The assumption was that I did not eat meat. Indeed, that assumption was clearly stamped into the questioner's facial expression. So regular was this inquiry that I developed a complex over the fact that I was not a vegetarian. When the dreaded question came, I would flinch and break into a stuttering, embarrassed explanation.

"Oh, well, no—well, actually, not yes, that is—but I don't eat red meat."

It was a mixture of self-deceit, guilt, and justification. It seemed grossly unfair that just because I had some insight and experience with the spirit of Nature, it should be assumed I was a vegetarian.

One evening, after a talk about sensitivity in relating to Nature, I was invited to visit the gallery of a very gifted artist the following afternoon.

Soon after Treenie and I arrived, and while we were admiring some of her work and talking about things in general, the artist asked, "Of course, you are a vegetarian, aren't you?"

There was no way I could avoid it. Taking a deep breath, I gave it my best shot. "Er, well, no, actually I'm not."

The artist stood facing me, stunned, then she took an involuntary step back as though I were contaminated.

"But how can you bear to eat decaying flesh?" she asked incredulously.

For the first time, I stood my ground on this volatile and provocative issue. Besides, there was no place to run! "How is decaying flesh any different from decaying fruit or vegetables? Plants are not so different from animals; they also have consciousness. Surely it is just as good to eat meat and vegetables with a silent prayer and inner awareness as it is to eat only vegetables with the blind assumption that it is the one true way."

I got really steamed up as all my suppressed emotions on this issue came tumbling out. "I believe the key to whatever we eat is inner awareness of it as food. Why categorize

188

it as good and bad? Why not leave it to individual choice? Nature doesn't condemn the carnivore and rejoice in the herbivore. To me, the issue is not what I eat, but the way what I eat is produced. Both meat and vegetables are produced under the most appalling, unnatural conditions. I exercise my awareness by choosing to buy meat and vegetables that are grown under natural, chemical-free conditions. That's where it's at for me."

I paused to get my breath. I stared around at the blank, shocked faces. "Frankly, it seems to me that what goes into the mouth might not be so important as what comes out."

The artist's husband had been listening to my lengthy outburst. "So if we eat organic human flesh with awareness, that is all right?" he asked in a voice dripping with contempt.

It was truly a wonderful moment. His extreme attitude was so far over the top it enabled me to burst through all my previous justification and be true to myself. There was nothing more that needed to be said. I took Treenie's hand, we walked to the car, got in, and drove away.

What is truly fascinating is that once I had surmounted this problem and come to terms with myself and the way I am, only very rarely was I asked that question again.

❀　　❀　　❀

Being true to yourself takes more than personal courage. You also need to know who you are. Only then can you know whom to be true to.

A number of years ago, Treenie and I were on our way back from the inner city, traveling on a steetcar in Melbourne, Oz. The ticket collector struck me as an eccentric

type, and on observing him I realized that he was an on-
going reflection of his passengers.

Taking a ticket from a pretty, smiling girl, his eyes sparkled,
covertly flirting with her. Moments later, a grumpy old man
caused him to be gruff and abrupt, only to change again
when a tiny, elderly woman drew some charm and gallan-
try from him. He was truly a human chameleon!

After the tickets were taken, one elderly man hung
dithering near the door, trying to decide where to get off.
He waited too long. The streetcar was just moving from
its stop when he jumped forward and promptly fell out
of the open door.

Staggering to his feet at the roadside, his face mottled
with rage and humiliation, the old man hurled foul abuse
at the receding car. Almost beside himself with fury, the
ticket collector hung out the door screaming expletives
back.

Only another couple of uneventful stops and it was our
turn to depart. As we got up from our seats, I turned to
the collector. "Thank you for such an interesting ride. You
sure get all types of people on here."

For a moment he looked thunderstruck, his jaw slack
in astonishment. A look of suspicion entered his eyes. I
gave him a genuine smile, and suddenly his inner light
switched on. "Thank you, sir, thank you. Have a good day."
When I left him, he was in a definite state of well-being.

The point of this story is power. In each encounter, the
ticket collector unintentionally gave away his power. He
changed according to the state of each passenger he had
an exchange with. He became a victim of each of their

moods. The conductor had an undeveloped sense of self. He had no center. In fact, at the end of a day like the one we had observed, he would be scattered and fragmented—unstable. If he continued in that way, he would become yet another stressed patient in a mental health clinic. He did not know himself well enough to know who to be true to!

Other people's stress and anger need not become our own. One late afternoon in Sydney, Oz, during rush hour, I pulled up at a set of traffic lights. I had my right indicator blinking long before I noticed the no-right-turn sign. However, just as I did see it, a car pulled up on my right. The window rapidly slid down, revealing a snarling face. The face then proceeded to question my birthright! And, would you believe it, my parents' sexual habits! All because I proposed to turn right when I should not.

When he had finished his tirade, I smiled at him, all teeth. "And a very good day to you, too," I called out as the lights changed and I drove straight ahead. In his fury, he stalled his engine, creating a cacophony of car horn blasts from other, equally impatient drivers behind him.

To thine own self be true. It's simple, powerful, and sometimes fun!

31

A Parisian Encounter

I really enjoy the moments of serendipity, when magical chance weaves its wondrous design into our lives. I named our home Serendipity because of the way it found us, but the joke is I do not believe in chance. I subscribe to nothing by accident, nothing by chance. The seeds of empowerment lie within this, while chance suggests we have little or no control in the design of our lives.

However, this is not to debate a point, but rather to share one of those moments of serendipity.

Treenie and I were in England for three months, just prior to our tour of the United States. We were spending a weekend with my brother, Christopher, and my niece Cecelia, when Christopher casually mentioned that he would be in Paris the week before Christmas. Knowing that Treenie would enjoy it, I asked if we could go along. Christopher was delighted, and the arrangements were made. We also invited Christine, his au pair, who was born in Paris and was here for a year studying at Cambridge University.

Following a day of violent winds and rain, we set off on a Sunday evening to catch the midnight ferry from Dover. At the terminal, we joined one of the many lines of traffic already forming. Apparently, there had been no shipping that day; we watched truck after truck trundle onto the ferry, wondering if there would be room for us, but we made it. Only five more cars squeezed on after us.

Apart from a bit of pitch and toss, our crossing was uneventful. When we arrived at Calais, we were impatiently waved through customs, our passports unchecked. Christopher then drove through the night, heading for Paris at his usual breakneck speed.

We arrived in Paris around 5:00 A.M., but it took another half hour to find a parking place. Parking in Paris is quite an education. Cars were parked in every available space, as well as in spaces that were not available, including the pavement. When we eventually found an impossible space of our own, I learned the astonishing method of parking whereby you edge your way between two cars by actually bumper pushing them out of the way in front and behind you. Christopher did it brilliantly. Personally, I think he enjoyed it.

We checked into a small hotel, washed and freshened up, and were about to leave for breakfast, when the concierge suggested to Christine that we might like to eat there. At about this stage, I discovered that Parisians, whether or not they can speak English, only speak in French. Although Christopher spoke the language well, I was already thankful that Christine would be our guide and interpreter.

We sat down to a French breakfast, served directly onto the marble table instead of on plates. This, of course, was not a bacon and eggs meal, but croissants and French bread, with butter and jam.

While this enjoyable fast breaking was taking place, a

woman had come down from her room and been seated at a table close by. I noticed that she kept staring at me, a deep and speculative gaze. Eventually, she got up and approached Christine, having concluded that here was a compatriot. For a while they chatted in French, frequently glancing at me and at Treenie. Finally, while the woman stood beaming, Christine told us that she had been in the city yesterday browsing in a bookshop and had come across a book entitled *Dialogue avec la nature*. She had brought it home, read it during the evening and that night, and then fell asleep. On waking, she had meditated on the book, and her one deep desire had been to meet the author. She had seen a picture of the author and his wife in the book; to her astonishment and delight, she was sure that we were they. Was this so? Christine had assured her she was right. The book was the French version of *Talking With Nature*.

My dear brother was dumbfounded. "This is absolutely incredible. Such a coincidence isn't possible. I just don't believe it." And other such remarks.

The language may have been limiting, but hugs and kisses and laughter also say a lot. For Treenie and me, there was a deeper joke in this. When I first got an American publisher, I decided not to have my photograph in my books. The French publishers, however, insisted on one of me, and one of me and Treenie together. Exasperated, I had agreed, saying to Treenie, "Okay, what does it matter? Nobody in France is ever likely to see us, never mind recognize us."

We had been recognized almost immediately. But then, I do believe the universe enjoys a serendipitous joke!

32

The Last Letter

One of the more subtle areas of my development has been my intuition. We all have intuition, but we are not all prepared to trust it. Generally speaking, women trust their intuitive powers more than men. Perhaps it's intuitive; it's certainly intelligent. Men seem more pragmatic. Intuition stems directly from our simplicity, from our ability to bypass the clutter of the mind and reach directly into our innate sense of knowing.

I remember once when I was a teenager, a friend of mine discovered that the spare tire of his car was flat. He had an important first date that evening and knew he should take the spare around to the garage immediately, but he was busy. He reasoned that as he had not had a puncture in two years of fairly intensive driving, it was unlikely he would get one tonight. At the same time, deep inside, his intuition told him that he *would* get a puncture that night.

He dismissed intuition and followed reason. You guessed it — he got a flat and missed his important date. The good news is his girl forgave him, and later married him.

The everyday incidents that could teach us to trust our intuition are often so trivial we dismiss them. We overlook the fact that by the nature of its simplicity we lose sight of intuition's power. A good example is when Treenie and I went shopping at a new plaza a few years ago. As we walked into the huge complex, a fish shop at the entrance caught my eye. I walked over, and there on a display slab was a large pile of fresh school prawns. My mouth watered at the sight of them.

"I'll go in and get some," I said to Treenie.

"Wait," she replied. "You don't want to carry them around for the next half hour. Wait until we are about to leave."

Very logical, very sensible. But my intuition informed me that in half an hour the prawns would all be sold. "They might be sold out by then," I replied, without much conviction.

"Of course they won't. Not a big pile like that."

My intuition still insisted that they would definitely be sold out, but I dismissed it. After all, I reasoned, Treenie is always right.

Of course, you know what happened. When we came out half an hour later, not a prawn remained. I even went into the shop to ask if there were any hidden ones left. "Sorry, mate. We had plenty half an hour ago, then there was a sudden run on them," the shopkeeper told me.

I came out of the shop and glared at Treenie. "See! I knew they would be sold out. It's all your fault! My intuition told me they would be sold, but I listened to you instead!"

Treenie smiled at me sweetly. "Sorry, my darling, but we both know better. You should always trust your intuition. That was your lesson. You should always trust your self."

So I had to swallow that—instead of prawns!

Intuition is not, nor should it ever be considered, a minor ability. Intuition is our self, speaking from the heart, quietly trying to penetrate the incessant chatter of the mind. What intuition has to say, or tries to prompt, can be very important, as in those documented cases of people who, having booked a flight, declined to enter the plane prior to take off, because, overwhelmingly, their intuition said not to. And the plane crashed!

I'd like to share another incident, not particularly dramatic or life threatening, but in retrospect one that makes me very glad I followed my intuition.

To tell the story requires that I go back into my boyhood to introduce the central character, Miss Kitty Willers. She taught me to ring the church bells when I was a boy, a practice I enjoyed for ten years. When, with other boys, I used to "ring the bells down" and then swing on the ropes of the huge bells like a boy Tarzan, she would smile tolerantly. Kitty Willers was patience and goodness personified, a rare and remarkable woman. No matter what mischief I got into, she never got angry, never lost her temper. And I gave her some wonderful opportunities! One evening, I got to church for bell-ringing practice ahead of the other boys. When they arrived, I held the huge, old, iron-bound oak door shut against them. So thick was the wood of the door that their pounding and shouting was muffled. Eventually, after ten delightful minutes, I snatched the door open. To my horror, the first person to pitch headfirst through the door and sprawl on the floor in an untidy heap of brown wool stockings and frilly petticoats was Kitty Willers. Even then, she quickly forgave me.

Kitty Willers devoted her life to the church, her father, and other people. Most of her time was spent making gloves, hats, wallets and purses, and a range of leather items, mostly using rabbit skins. All this to be sold at a once-a-year sale for church funds. People stood in line for hours waiting to get an early choice, such was her reputation. She was an eccentric, wearing long skirts and knee-length pantaloon knickers for all seasons. Her hair was invariably in a severe bun, and I never saw her look anything other than around fifty years old. When, in her early seventies, she bought a Vespa motor scooter and took off on a tour of Scotland ringing the church bells as she visited each parish, none of those who really knew her were surprised. Kitty Willers was an exceptional woman.

After I emigrated from England, at least twenty years passed without my seeing her. I was in Oz one Christmas day, when thoughts and memories of Kitty Willers surged unbidden into my mind. I knew from my mother's letters that Kitty Willers was still alive, and that her father had long since died. I realized that Kitty would have to be a very old lady by now. As strongly as I have ever felt it, intuition urged me to write to Kitty Willers, and share with her just what she had meant to me in my life. Having never written to her before, I resisted, but the inner bidding was relentless. I told Treenie, hoping she would laugh it away. She did not. "I definitely think you should write to her," she said seriously.

So I did. I sat down and wrote a long, careful letter sharing some of the incidents I remembered. I told her how her unfailing goodness and strength of character had so deeply impressed me, how I had inadvertently used her as a role model for my own measure of character. I thanked her for being such an inspiration in my life. I told her that

200

in all my life, only she and my Aunt Polly had ever epitomized all the very best in humanity. I told her how much
I appreciated her, and how she had enriched my youth
simply by being herself. I even told her that I loved her.

In this vein, I wrote, sharing my heart, for there is no
other way I know of writing. After the letter was sealed
and posted, I felt embarrassed, almost regretting the way
I had laid bare my feelings for her.

I never heard from Kitty Willers. However, about a month
after I sent my letter, my mother wrote to me that Miss
Willers had been found dead sitting on the stairs in her
house. She had been dead for about two days.

Somehow I knew that as her time closed in, Kitty Willers
had been reassessing her life, maybe questioning whether
the way she had lived it had been of value. Intuitively, I
knew that she had been at a low point, needing some sort
of human recognition, some form of acknowledgment. She
had no family, no one at all. Undoubtedly, she was very
lonely in her advanced years. That she believed in God was
never in question. But I think that this extraordinary, gentle
woman, who had never in her life been known to voice a
negative comment about anyone, was questioning God
about her own self-worth. To this day, I believe that God answered her through my letter—a letter of love and appreciation for all that she was, a recognition of all that she had
expressed in her life, a letter of personal empowerment
when it was most needed. I wouldn't mind betting that mine
was the last letter, maybe the last words, she ever read.

Why am I so sure? Because, overwhelmingly, my intuition tells me so. And I am simple enough to trust it.

A Request

Having read the stories in this book, undoubtedly you have recalled some simple but powerful moments, moments that have changed your life, either subtly or dramatically. The moment of empowerment may have been personal; perhaps it involved your relationship with Nature, or your family, but it was a turning point in your life.

I am interested in your *true* story that is simple and powerful. If you have such a moment in your life that you are willing to share with others for their empowerment, please send it to me. I would prefer it typed. It is my intention to compile a book of other "simple is powerful" stories. By sending me your story, you grant permission for its publication if it is selected. I will send a free signed copy of the finished book to each person who has a story in it. My address is: Michael J. Roads

P.O. Box 778

Nambour, Queensland

Australia 4560

Accompanied by Treenie, I travel extensively giving public talks on the many themes contained in *Simple Is Powerful*. Organizations or persons interested can contact us at the above address.

For those people who want information concerning the Homeland commune, please be aware that I left there long ago and I am no longer involved with them in any way. Any inquiries should be directed to them. Their address is:

The Homeland Foundation
Thora, Bellingen
New South Wales 2454 Australia

COMPATIBLE BOOKS

FROM H J KRAMER INC

TALKING WITH NATURE
by Michael J. Roads
"From Australia comes a major new writer . . . a magnificent book!"
—RICHARD BACH, Author, *Jonathan Livingston Seagull*

JOURNEY INTO NATURE: A SPIRITUAL ADVENTURE
by Michael J. Roads
"If you only read one book this year, make that book
JOURNEY INTO NATURE."—*Friend's Review*

WAY OF THE PEACEFUL WARRIOR
by Dan Millman
A tale of transformation and adventure . . . a worldwide best-seller.

SACRED JOURNEY OF THE PEACEFUL WARRIOR
by Dan Millman
The eagerly awaited sequel to the international best-selling
WAY OF THE PEACEFUL WARRIOR.

An Orin/DaBen Book
CREATING MONEY
by Sanaya Roman and Duane Packer, Ph.D.
This best-selling book teaches advanced manifesting techniques.

IN SEARCH OF BALANCE
by John Robbins and Ann Mortifee
An inquiry into issues and concerns of the heart from the
best-selling author of DIET FOR A NEW AMERICA.

MESSENGERS OF LIGHT:
THE ANGELS' GUIDE TO SPIRITUAL GROWTH
by Terry Lynn Taylor
At last, a practical way to connect with the
angels and to bring heaven into your life!

UNDERSTAND YOUR DREAMS
by Alice Anne Parker
A practical book that offers the reader
the key to dream interpretation.

COMPATIBLE BOOKS

FROM H J KRAMER INC

THE EARTH LIFE SERIES
by Sanaya Roman
*A course in learning to live with joy,
sense energy, and grow spiritually.*

LIVING WITH JOY, BOOK I
*"I like this book because it describes the way I feel about
so many things."* —VIRGINIA SATIR

PERSONAL POWER THROUGH AWARENESS:
A GUIDEBOOK FOR SENSITIVE PEOPLE, BOOK II
"Every sentence contains a pearl. . . ." —LILIAS FOLAN

SPIRITUAL GROWTH:
BEING YOUR HIGHER SELF, BOOK III
*Orin teaches how to reach upward to align with the
higher energies of the universe, look inward to expand
awareness, and move outward in world service.*

EAT FOR HEALTH:
FAST AND SIMPLE WAYS OF ELIMINATING
DISEASES WITHOUT MEDICAL ASSISTANCE
by William Manahan, M.D.
"Essential reading and an outstanding selection." —*Library Journal*

AMAZING GRAINS: CREATING VEGETARIAN
MAIN DISHES WITH WHOLE GRAINS
by Joanne Saltzman
*AMAZING GRAINS is really two books in one, a book of recipes
and a book that teaches the creative process in cooking.*

SEVENFOLD PEACE
by Gabriel Cousens, M.D.
*A book that expands our awareness of peace so that
we may all contribute to create a world at peace.*

THE PERSECUTION AND TRIAL
OF GASTON NAESSENS
by Christopher Bird
*The true story of the efforts to suppress an alternative treatment
for cancer, AIDS, and other immunologically based diseases.*